Asset Protection
for Everyone

Asset Protection for Everyone

Secrets to Legally Safeguarding Your Hard-Earned Money, Home & Business

B. Roland Frasier, III

Sourcebooks Inc.

Naperville, IL

Published by: Sourcebooks, Inc.

P.O. Box 372
Naperville, Illinois 60566
(630) 961-3900
FAX: 630-961-2168

This publication is designed to provide accurate and authoritative information in regard to the subject matter covered. It is sold with the understanding that the publisher is not engaged in rendering legal, accounting, or other professional service. If legal advice or other expert assistance is required, the services of a competent professional person should be sought.

From a Declaration of Principles Jointly Adopted by a Committee of the American Bar Association and a Committee of Publishers and Associations

Library of Congress Cataloging-in-Publication Data
Frasier, B. Roland
    Asset protection for everyone: secrets to legally safeguarding your
  hard-earned money, home & business / B. Roland Frasier III.
        p.   cm.
    Includes index.
    ISBN 1-57071-128-3
    1. Executions (Law)—United States—Popular works.   2. Debtor and
  creditor—United States—Popular works.   3. Limited liability—United
  States—Popular works.   4. Estate planning—United States.
  I. Title.
  KF9025.Z9F73   1997
  346.7307'7—dc21   97-26545
                                                              CIP

Printed and bound in the United States of America.
    Paperback — 10 9 8 7 6 5 4 3 2 1

For Lynne

Table of Contents

Asset Protection
for Everyone

Introduction

Blame It on Litigation

Over the past few years, the rising tide of frivolous litigation filed by plaintiffs and their lawyers has created a new trend for those who once considered their assets relatively safe from creditor claims. Insurance, once a viable asset protection alternative, has proved an inadequate sentry at the gate of your wealth, as even once strong insurance companies have crumbled under the relentless assault of the army of litigants making claims against their policy holders.

Incorporation is another liability-limiting tool that once served to thwart the arrows shot by those attacking your hard-earned wealth, but modern jury verdicts and bad case law have eroded much of the benefit of corporate asset protection. This erosion results from permitting claims under theories of under-capitalization, commingling corporate assets with personal assets, failure to follow corporate formalities, and public policy arguments. The net result is that simply doing business as a corporation no longer assures that your wealth will be protected from the claims of those seeking recovery against your personal assets.

What does all this mean? Is it simply impossible to protect yourself from creditors these days? Should you abandon your American dream of working hard to create a nest egg and retire, because you will need to save enough additional money to fund expensive lawsuits and settlements for mistakes you may have made in the past or accidents that you may have in the future? The answer is "not necessarily."

Asset Protection Is the Answer

Through careful attention to how you structure the ownership of your assets and proper planning, you can amass personal wealth and protect it from the grasping claws of your creditors, even government creditors like the Internal Revenue Service and state taxing agencies. The key to successful asset protection planning is "planning." You must start NOW to protect the assets you have and to create a structure that will grow with you as you accumulate more and more assets in the future.

You Must Plan before a Lawsuit Is Filed

If you wait until you are a defendant in a lawsuit, your options become extremely limited because there are numerous state and federal laws (which we will discuss later) designed to stop people from transferring or protecting assets from creditors who are readily identifiable and who have legitimate existing claims against someone. The time to do your planning is *before* these creditors are known, before they have any claims they could assert against you and your assets. This advance planning can offer complete protection for your wealth and provide a great deal of peace of mind.

Four Fronts on Which to Defend Your Assets

Planning generally consists of protection on several fronts, including the following:

- structuring your affairs so that you are an unattractive target for a plaintiff or lawyer who might consider taking a case against you on a contingency basis

- acquiring and maintaining adequate insurance to cover realistic risks to your wealth (such as automobile, casualty, homeowner's, errors and omissions, and general comprehensive liability insurance)

- placing your assets in debtor friendly / creditor hostile entities so that you make an unappealing target in the sites of a judgment creditor

- keeping a low profile by avoiding owning or displaying expensive houses, exotic cars or flashy jewelry

Failure to address any one of these areas will not necessarily result in the loss of your assets in the face of a creditor claim. But, isn't it smart to have all the protection you can considering the risk of losing everything you own to a creditor you never thought you would have? Keep in mind that the objective of asset protection planning is to provide as much protection as possible to the assets that you have. If you take too many risks, or if you aren't committed to taking the steps necessary to protect your wealth, then it's up for grabs for any creditor or contingency fee lawyer who wants to take a shot at it. You've taken the first step by purchasing this book. Be sure that you follow through and put the strategies and techniques it provides to use for you as soon as possible.

As an attorney practicing in the areas of asset protection, taxation, business, and estate planning, I have assisted hundreds of clients in protecting their assets. From builders and developers to movie stars and well-known entertainment personalities, I have designed and implemented plans to protect the wealth that my clients accumulated from unfounded claims. In doing so, I typically charge $25,000–$100,000 for complete asset protection plans. In this book, I will explain to you the secrets I have learned during the course of my legal career, and I will provide you with a step-by-step, easy to understand guide on how to protect your assets using the proven strategies I have developed and honed—all for the price of this book.

Whether you're a new homeowner trying to figure out how to protect the equity in your home, a small business owner trying to protect your business, or a world-class billionaire requiring a complex plan, this book contains everything you need to know to design and implement the right plan to protect your assets. Some of the topics and plans presented in this book may not be right for your particular situation, but there is something here for everyone who believes that it is time to take action to protect their wealth.

Disclaimers and Other Legal Mumbo Jumbo

Keep in mind that while this book provides a guide to protecting your assets, the laws vary from state to state, and laws governing asset protection are in a constant state of change. Therefore, it is a good idea to use the information provided in this book as a starting point for your asset protection plan.

Before finalizing your plan, however, you should contact and consult with a qualified attorney who is experienced in the areas of asset protection planning; income, estate and gift taxation; and bankruptcy and creditors rights laws. The best asset protection plan in the world won't do you any good if it runs afoul of the law.

As you read through the following chapters, keep in mind that this book is intended to cover complex procedures. You will be able to understand and implement many of the ideas, strategies, and techniques yourself. However, the subject matter contained in this book is intended for instructional purposes only. If legal or other expert advice is required, you should seek the services of competent professionals.

Although much care has been taken to ensure the accuracy and adaptability of the information provided in this book, the author assumes no liability to any party for loss or damages caused by errors or omissions contained in this book whether such errors or omissions are the result of negligence or otherwise. Additionally, the author makes no warranty that the suggestions and/or recommendations contained in this book are suitable for all readers.

Chapter Highlights

Chapter One discusses what asset protection is and why you need it. It describes the flood of litigation and why it shows no signs of letting up. It then explains why lawyers look for defendants with "deep pockets" to file lawsuits against. The chapter then moves on to talk about who should consider asset protection planning and what role professionals can and should play in designing and implementing your plan.

Protection from government and other creditors is then discussed, as is just how much asset protection you need. The chapter ends with a description of the advantages and disadvantages of asset protection planning, commonly asked questions with answers, and a quick quiz to help you determine whether asset protection is right for you.

Chapter Two discusses the legal aspects of asset protection planning. It begins by asking the question, how much of your wealth can you legally protect? It then goes on to discuss the difference between potential creditors and future creditors and which type of creditors you can protect your assets from. The chapter then explains the fraudulent conveyances laws and why it is important to protect your assets before lawsuits are threatened or filed. Badges of fraud are examined next, with a brief description of what situations may lead a court to infer fraudulent intent in connection with your asset protection planning.

Chapter Two also discusses asset protection in the context of the bankruptcy laws, before examining the applicability of money laundering, technology transfer restriction, and public policy boycott laws to your planning. The chapter wraps up with a discussion of the major tax reporting and compliance issues presented by asset protection planning, questions and answers about the limitations on asset protection planning, and a quick quiz to help you determine whether you can qualify for asset protection planning.

Chapter Three discusses strategies and techniques for dealing with creditors, both before and after they have filed suit. The chapter discusses how to settle disputes with creditors, provides sample clauses to use in settlement agreements, briefly explains creditors' rights, and provides sample questions that creditors or their attorneys might ask you if you were ever subpoenaed to testify at a debtor's examination proceeding.

Chapter Four discusses how to protect your home and other important assets with little or no effort by using state and federal laws. We will examine homesteads and the steps you need to take to gain homestead protection if it is available in your state, including ten action steps to maximize your homestead protection benefits. The chapter then goes on to show how to protect your retirement savings, insurance, and annuities.

Chapter Five shows how to use partnerships to protect your personal assets. It begins with a discussion of why partnerships provide protection for your personal assets and then discusses the use and role of family limited partnerships in asset protection planning.

The structure and ownership of a family limited partnership are then discussed, along with drafting considerations, how to transfer assets to the partnership, valuation, and estate planning issues. The chapter concludes with questions and answers about family limited partnerships and partnerships in asset protection planning, and a quick quiz to help you determine whether a family limited partnership is right for you.

Chapter Six discusses the use of domestic corporations and limited liability companies (LLCs) for the protection of your business assets. We will first look at the major advantages of corporations and the major advantages of LLCs, and the differences between these two types of entities. Tax reduction is then addressed in the context of the "bracket game" and the use of multiple corporations or LLCs to reduce the total amount of income taxes that you pay. There are weaknesses to any planning tool, and corporations are no exception, as you will learn later when we discuss corporations.

Chapter Six then moves on to discuss how to use corporations and LLCs to reduce your state income taxes, a strategy that can save you tens of thousands of dollars over only a few short years. The chapter then discusses where to incorporate to maximize asset protection and tax benefits, how to use corporations and LLCs to reduce estate taxes, and the benefits of professional and non-profit corporations. We conclude with questions and answers about corporations and LLCs and a quick quiz to help you determine whether you should use a corporation or LLC in your personal asset protection plan.

Chapter Seven discusses the use of foreign corporations in asset protection planning and how they can provide even greater protection of your personal and business assets than partnerships and domestic entities. The chapter begins with a discussion of how foreign corporations can bulletproof your assets and how to pick the right country for your foreign corporation. The advantages and disadvantages of using a foreign corporation are then discussed, along with how foreign corporations can fit into your overall plan.

We will then examine how to use foreign corporations to reduce taxes on both your international and United States based income, as well as estate, gift, and generation-skipping transfer taxes. The chapter concludes with suggestions on the use of nominee officers and directors, questions and answers about foreign corporations, and a quick quiz to help you determine whether you should use a foreign corporation in your asset protection plan.

Chapter Eight discusses the use of both foreign and domestic trusts in your asset protection plan. It begins by discussing how trusts can be used to provide even greater asset protection planning benefits than corporations, and why living trusts provide little if any asset protection. We will compare and contrast revocable and irrevocable trusts and look at the differences between domestic and foreign trusts.

Chapter Eight then suggests which countries you should consider when forming a foreign asset protection trust. We will also cover how to use fictitious name trusts, sprinkling trusts, and nominee trustees to reduce your exposure to liability. The chapter concludes with questions and answers about using trusts in your asset protection plan and a quick quiz to help you determine whether a trust is right for your plan, and if so, what kind.

Chapter Nine presents a brief discussion of the advantages and disadvantages of most of the major and most popular offshore financial centers used in asset protection planning. After discussing each of the best jurisdictions, you can contact me directly to learn the names and addresses of local contacts to assist you in interviewing and price shopping service providers.

Chapter Ten provides several flowcharts of sample asset protection plan structures and designs. Plans include: 1) simple domestic plan to protect a family home, 2) simple domestic plan for an unmarried person, 3) simple domestic plan for married couple without children, 4) simple domestic plan for married couple with children, 5) simple domestic plan for a business owner, 6) complex foreign plan to protect a family home, 7) complex foreign plan for an unmarried person, 8) complex foreign plan for a married couple without children, 9) complex foreign plan for a married couple with children, 10) complex foreign plan for a business owner, 11) state income tax reduction plan, 12) state and federal income tax reduction plan, 13) estate tax reduction plan, 14) plan for intellectual property owners, 15) plan for those engaged in high risk occupations, 16) plan for celebrities, 17) plan for stock promoters and investment advisors, 18) plan for doctors and 19) a plan for attorneys.

Chapter Eleven offers tips for managing your asset protection plan after implementation and how to keep it funded and protected. It begins by discussing how to manage the plan once it is formed, how to transfer assets to the plan, and how to invest from within the plan without losing its asset protection benefits. The chapter then discusses how to defend the plan from attacks by creditors and how to keep up with changing treaties and laws. Finally, we conclude with a discussion of regular tax and related reporting compliance.

Chapter Twelve will help you tie all of the information you have gathered together and tell you where to get more information to assist you in your quest to design and implement an asset protection plan that's right for you. Now, let's get started.

Chapter One

What Is Asset Protection and Why Do You Need It?

Many people are confused as to just what asset protection means. Some think it's what mobsters and criminals do to keep one step ahead of the law, while others have visions of elaborate offshore schemes involving wire transfers among multiple bank accounts located throughout various exotic Asian and Caribbean countries. While these scenarios are indeed possible forms of asset protection, few people require such elaborate schemes to adequately protect their wealth.

A Working Definition

In fact, asset protection can be as simple as buying an insurance policy or incorporating a business. Despite all the hype in the media about asset protection, it's really nothing new. It is a logical result of more people consciously thinking about the benefits of planning to protect their assets.

Today's heightened concern about asset protection results from the devastation caused when those who have planned for their future and accumulated wealth lose it all to creditors they never knew existed. For purposes of this book, asset protection simply means taking steps to preserve your wealth.

What Asset Protection Isn't

Asset protection is not a way to avoid accountability for intentional or criminal acts. As you'll see later in the sections on fraud, criminal penalties, and contempt, there are many laws to prevent this misuse of asset protection planning. Similarly, it is not a way to escape liability for your past actions. The same laws that stop criminals from misusing asset protection planning also apply to attempts to transfer assets to friendly parties in the face of pending or

...asset protection simply means taking steps to preserve your wealth.

threatened litigation. Generally, asset protection planning is like getting a bank loan: you can't get it when you need it, but it's easy to get if you don't.

When You Should Start to Protect Your Assets

The best time to consider asset protection planning is before you need it. If a lawsuit has already been filed, there are certain steps you may take without running afoul of the law, but your planning options are extremely limited. On the other hand, if you begin your asset protection planning before your creditors become a problem and before any suits are threatened or filed, then your options are only limited by your creativity and your ability to retain enough assets to satisfy existing liabilities and debts as they come due. The time to start planning is now.

A Flood of Litigation Drowning the American Dream

Over the past several years the number of lawsuits filed in the United States has increased dramatically. Some statistics estimate that five new lawsuits are filed in this country every minute of each day. That's a lot of lawsuits! Other statistics say that you have almost a 100 percent chance of being hit with some sort of lawsuit during your lifetime.

...five new lawsuits are filed in this country every minute of each day...you have almost a 100 percent chance of being hit with some sort of lawsuit during your lifetime.

These lawsuits aren't limited to claims against the wealthy either. Rarely is someone involved in a car accident where they don't consult with a lawyer to see how much they can get from the insurance company, whether the driver has money or not. Also, many lawyers are only too willing to accept weak cases if they suspect the possibility of a big settlement from an insurance company.

Lawyers' aggressive behavior is based on the fact that most personal injury lawyers are paid on a contingency basis. They receive a portion of the recovery they obtain from the defendant, or more likely, from the defendant's insurance company. While it is true that the attorney generally recovers no fee unless the case is won, a general rule of thumb is that a personal injury plaintiff will recover three times the medical damages if the case goes to trial. Based on this rule of thumb, most insurance companies simply settle claims against their policy holders. If the lawyer knows that the "meds" are good, there is little risk of non-payment in taking a contingency fee case.

These trends are not threatening if you have adequate insurance, but what if your insurance policy limits are *exceeded* by an award based on some formula like the three times "meds" formula? Your insurance company is generally permitted to settle the case with the other side for the policy limits, leaving you out in the cold on the difference. While that might not seem fair, it is how most modern auto insurance policies are written, and it doesn't offer much protection to someone trying to minimize the high cost of insurance by lowering coverage amounts and raising deductibles.

Fishing for Money in Deep Pockets

If you were on a camping trip fishing for your dinner, where would you drop your line? Would you drop it into a small, shallow stream filled with sticks and debris, or in a deep blue lake brimming with fish? Obviously, you would choose the lake. Lawyers choose who they are going to sue in much the same way. If they risk accepting a case on a contingency basis, then they're going to fish for their fees in the deepest pockets they can find. The deeper the pocket, the more intense the lawyers' resolve to catch a fee.

Armed with this knowledge, it is evident that to avoid having a contingency fee lawyer drop a line into your pocket, simply structure your affairs so that it looks like you're a little fish. Just as you would avoid the little stream in favor of the big lake, the lawyer will avoid a shallow pocket filled with unattractive assets. If it looks like the fight is going to be more trouble than it's worth, the lawyer will go looking somewhere else to cast a line.

...structure your affairs so that it looks like you're a little fish.

On the other hand, if you drive exotic sports cars, live in a million dollar house, and wear a Rolex watch, the contingency fee lawyer will be very eager to go fishing.

A Case in Point

Consider a case our law firm took on contingency not too long ago. A client came to us with a case against a contractor who the client hired to do major remodeling work on the client's house. The contractor botched the job, leaving the client with a house that couldn't be lived in and damages of more than $200,000.

We performed an asset search to see if the developer had any personal assets that would make the case worth taking on a contingency basis. The search revealed that the contractor owned a million dollar home with about $600,000 of equity, several sports cars, and other attractive assets. We took the case.

We had two major obstacles to overcome to get to the assets we identified in our asset search. First, the contractor did business as a corporation, so we would have to "pierce" the corporation to recover against his personal assets if we got a judgment. The second obstacle was a provision the contractor had placed in his contract limiting his total liability for any mistakes made in performing his contracting services to the amount of the contract, in this case $50,000.

Eventually, we overcame the first obstacle by convincing the court that the contractor had consented to being sued personally, and therefore waived any argument that he should not be sued as an individual. We overcame the second obstacle by making public policy arguments as to why it was not in the interest of society to permit rich, negligent contractors to take money from helpless consumers, completely demolish their homes, and claim that their liability should be limited to the amount of the contract.

With all of the contractor's defenses out of the way, the contractor threw in the towel and settled favorably for our client. He was virtually wiped out despite his carefully crafted plan to limit his personal exposure to lawsuits through a corporation and a contract with a limitation of damages clause.

Lessons Learned

Asset protection planning is very similar to net worth insurance.

This story offers many valuable lessons. First, if the contractor had maintained a lower profile, we would have been less likely to think he had enough money to make it worthwhile for us to take the case. Second, the contractor's asset protection plan relied on outdated and incomplete asset protection tools: a corporation and a limitation of liability clause. Third, the contractor didn't carry insurance to protect him because he thought it was too expensive. Had the he carried proper insurance, his policy probably would have picked up his legal fees and there would have been funds to settle the case that might have completely protected the contractor from personal liability for his negligence. The moral of this story: keep a low profile.

Who Should Consider Asset Protection

Anyone who wants to protect their assets from creditor claims needs asset protection planning. Whether you're a middle class family with two kids, two dogs, and a house; a small business owner who is just starting in business; a retired person living in a retirement facility with $100,000 in certificates of deposit; or a corporate executive with a million dollar a year income, it makes sense to learn about asset protection planning. Consider the following list of potential threats to your wealth as you think about whether you need to protect your assets.

Threats to Your Wealth

1. Unanticipated illness of yourself, a child or your spouse creating large medical bills not covered by your health insurance policy.

2. Bankruptcy of your insurance company or cancellation of your insurance policy due to too many claims or a change in underwriting policies by your insurance company.

3. An accident with an uninsured motorist where damages exceed your policy limits.

4. A tax audit by the Internal Revenue Service or a state taxing agency followed by a large assessment for taxes, penalties, and interest.

5. Divorce.

6. Bankruptcy or credit problems of one of your major customers, leaving you unable to pay your bills.

7. A forced layoff at your company.

8. A lawsuit for personal injuries suffered by someone visiting your business.

9. Negligence claims filed against you for improperly performing services or failing to properly supervise employees.

10. Sexual harassment suits or other claims filed against you as an employer.

How Much Protection Do You Need?

One of the questions most frequently asked in asset protection is just how much protection is needed. People want to take steps to protect their assets, but they don't want to do anything that would scare their mortgage lenders, create a red flag for the IRS that might lead to an audit, or cost tens of thousands of dollars.

The answer to this question is two-fold. First, you should have enough protection so that you feel comfortable that your assets are safe from the unreasonable claims of creditors, and that you are in a position to decide whether you are willing to part with any of those assets to satisfy a creditor's claim against you. Second, you should only implement an asset protection plan that you understand and that you feel is simple enough for you to follow on a continuing basis.

You can structure the ownership of your personal and business assets so that you never have to worry about losing them to the IRS or anyone else.

As you will see in the following chapters of this book, asset protection planning can range from the very simple to the extremely complex.

Advantages and Disadvantages of Asset Protection Planning

Table 1 briefly summarizes the general advantages and disadvantages of asset protection planning. Use it as a guide in determining whether you feel that asset protection planning is right for you.

Table 1
Advantages and Disadvantages of Asset Protection Planning

Type of Asset Protection	Advantage	Disadvantage
Homestead Protection	May protect up to the full amount of equity in your home. Easy to implement. Easy to maintain. Low cost.	Some lenders look unfavorably on those who file homesteads when considering loan applications.
General Partnership	Creditors have difficulty attaching partnership assets to satisfy claims against any individual partner. Moderately easy to implement. Moderately easy to maintain. Moderate cost.	Liability for acts of other partners where those acts occur in furtherance of the partnership's business. Requires more than one person to form, usually at least a trusted friend or relative beyond husband and wife. Additional tax filings and accounting.
Family Limited Partnerships, Corporations, and Limited Liability Companies	Permit segmentation of liability for various business and personal activities. Permit implementation of tax strategies not available in other forms of asset protection. Can be used to project a low profile, unattractive defendant image to creditors searching for deep pocket defendants.	Require filings with various government agencies. Additional tax filings and accounting. Complex implementation. Complex to maintain. Expensive.

Table 1 cont.

Type of Asset Protection	Advantage	Disadvantage
Trusts	Can provide maximum protection from creditors. Can provide estate planning and succession of wealth to heirs in accordance with your wishes. Can be used to project a low profile, unattractive defendant image to creditors searching for deep pocket defendants.	Require filings with various government agencies Additional tax filings and accounting. Complex implementation. Complex to maintain. Expensive.

Protecting Your Assets from the Government

One of the greatest potential threats to your assets is a claim by a state or federal government entity. Despite the general rule in this country that you are innocent until proven guilty, the Internal Revenue Service and most state and local government taxing agencies have the power to make you liable for taxes until you prove that you're not.

This power is even more formidable when you consider the fact that all these agencies have to do to get to your assets is to push the levy button on their computers. Yes, there really is a "levy" button! They simply determine that you owe them, send you a bill, and if you don't pay, they press the levy button and your assets are frozen until you either pay or prove that you don't owe them any money.

Even small businesses can face claims exceeding $100,000 for three or four years worth of taxes. Payment of these taxes could result in business closure, posing a threat to the owner's personal financial situation.

With proper asset protection planning, you can avoid the IRS and state taxing authority threat and place yourself in a much better position to negotiate a favorable settlement in the event a tax-related claim is made against you or your business.

Protecting Your Assets from Other Creditors

While the government is generally one of the biggest potential threats to your assets because of the incredible power it has to force you to pay taxes and other claims that you may not owe, other creditors can pose a significant threat as well.

Recently, multi-million dollar jury awards to plaintiffs who seemingly suffered little or no real damages have caused us to be much more aware of just how little protection we have in a society where you can be sued for almost anything.

For example, consider the person who spilled hot coffee on her lap and burned herself because she went through a fast food drive-thru and placed the coffee between her legs. She received a huge judgement because she claimed that the coffee was too hot.

Or, consider the secretary who worked for a law firm for less than a year at a salary of less than $50,000. She claimed that her immediate supervisor sexually harassed her and caused her to quit her job. She was able not only to recover against the supervisor for the sexual harassment, but she also received a multi-million dollar judgment against the supervisor's law firm because the jury determined that the law firm should have been more careful in protecting her.

Also consider the bank that repossessed a piece of real property from a defaulting borrower. It turned out that the land was environmentally contaminated and the bank was held liable under federal "superfund" environmental laws for millions of dollars in costs to clean up the property.

Any of these situations could easily happen to you or your business, and you could find yourself facing huge claims that would completely wipe out the wealth you have worked so hard to attain. You need to take action now, before creditors are standing on your doorstep with judgments in their hands.

Questions and Answers about Asset Protection

1. Q: *How much does it cost?*

   A: Simple asset protection strategies such as homestead filings can cost less than $10, while more complex plans involving multiple corporations and trusts can cost as much as $30,000 to establish, and several thousand dollars per year to maintain—even if you do all of the work yourself.

2. Q: *Should I hire an attorney or other professional advisor to help me with my asset protection planning?*

   A: It is generally a good idea to seek professional guidance at some point during the asset protection planning process. Most professionals will offer a free consultation during which you can bounce around several of the ideas and options that you learn from this book. You can use your free consultation to determine whether the person you are talking to seems familiar with asset protection planning principles and whether the chemistry is right to form a working relationship. The best way to use a professional advisor is to first create a plan that feels right to you by using this book, then take the plan to the advisor to tailor it to your particular situation and state laws.

3. Q: *If I don't want to hire anyone to help me with my asset protection plan, can I do it all myself?*
   A: Yes, but be sure that you research the applicable laws of your state to assure harmony between your plan, the agreements you create for the plan, and applicable state laws.

4. Q: *I've just been sued by someone. Can I transfer all of my assets to my wife or a friend?*
   A: Probably not. Most states have adopted laws that prohibit someone from transferring assets for less than their full fair market value where the purpose of the transfer is to delay or frustrate the ability of creditors to collect what is owed them.

5. Q: *I'm thinking of filing bankruptcy. Is asset protection another option?*
   A: It depends. Bankruptcy laws generally permit "pre-petition planning." Pre-petition planning is the process of rearranging your assets prior to filing a bankruptcy petition so that you can keep as many of them as possible despite the bankruptcy filing. State and federal laws provide that several types of assets are exempt from creditor claims. While these amounts are generally low, if you have a relatively small estate with limited assets, it is a good idea to determine whether the exemptions provided by your state will protect all or most of the assets that you have. If so, then you may not need to file bankruptcy. You may simply need to rearrange your assets to maximize your exemptions.

6. Q: *Is my pension safe from creditor claims?*
   A: It depends. Generally, most types of creditors other than IRS will be prevented from access to a public pension plan such as a 401(k), but they will generally be permitted to attach private pension plans such as IRAs and Keoghs. However, even if your pension plan is not completely exempt, you may still be able to protect it if you can prove that you need it for your retirement and there is little chance of replacing it considering your age, health, personal resources, and probable economic circumstances at the time of your retirement. If your pension plan does not qualify for exemption, consider switching to a plan that does, as it is extremely hard to meet the economic need test described above.

7. Q: *I'm thinking about going into a nursing home, and I want to qualify for any available state and federal support, but I know that there are limitations on those benefits based on income and net worth. Can I transfer or protect my assets to qualify for these benefits?*

A: Maybe. State laws vary, but many states have a "look back" period where any asset transfers for less than fair consideration during that period may be considered and may disqualify you from receiving state and federal benefits for some period of time, usually equal to the look back period. However, there still may be an advantage to spending down your estate to qualify for these benefits, even if you end up disqualifying yourself for the full look back period.

For example, assume you own a home worth about $100,000 that is completely paid for. Assume further that there is a three year look back period in your state for benefits which max out at $2,000 per month. In this situation, it probably makes sense to transfer the home to a family member and apply for benefits because the $72,000 ($2,000 per month x 3 years) of benefits, lost is still less than the $100,000 value of the house that was protected. Making the transfer saves you $28,000, and the proceeds from a home equity loan, sale, or reverse mortgage on the house can be used to pay the long-term care facility costs during the three year look back period during which no government assistance is received.

8. Q: *I already have a revocable living trust. What level of asset protection does that provide me?*

A: Virtually none. Your revocable living trust offers many estate planning advantages, but there are no real asset protection advantages afforded by a simple living trust.

9. Q: *Is asset protection legal?*

A: There is nothing wrong or illegal about asset protection planning when it is done properly. There are laws to prevent people from trying to escape liability from the claims of existing creditors, but proper asset protection planning is done prior to any such claims, and those laws do not apply to asset transfers which are not designed to cheat existing creditors.

10. Q: *My business is incorporated and insured. Won't that provide me with all of the asset protection I need?*

A: Probably not. As you read in the story about the building contractor earlier in this chapter, corporations offer increasingly less asset protection as waves of juries and courts continue to lap at the beachhead of limited liability once firmly established by the corporate form. The continual lapping of these waves has greatly eroded the protection afforded by corporations as cases have permitted the corporate liability veil to be pierced where the corporation was undercapitalized, corporate formalities were not followed, fraud is found, assets were commingled, or the corporation is determined to be the alter ego of its owners.

Insurance companies routinely deny coverage that they should honor out of their desire to maximize profits and limit losses, and as we have seen time and again, many insurance companies lack the stability to withstand several large claims or mismanage their assets so that they end up going bankrupt, leaving their faithful policy holders holding the bag. Additionally, most insurance policies do not cover willful acts such as fraud or intentional torts (a tort is a private wrong like assault-and-battery, false imprisonment, or copyright and trademark infringement).

Quick Quiz—Is Asset Protection Right for You?

The following exercise is a quick quiz to help you determine whether you can benefit from asset protection. Answer the questions and then add up the scores to see whether asset protection is right for you.

1. Do you own a home with equity of more than $25,000? __ Yes __ No

2. Do you have liquid stocks, bonds, or mutual funds valued at more than $25,000? __ Yes __ No

3. Is your net worth greater than $50,000? __ Yes __ No

4. Do you own your own business? __ Yes __ No

5. Do you have retirement savings greater than $25,000? __ Yes __ No

6. Do you have more than $10,000 in equity in your car? __ Yes __ No

7. Are you aware of any lawsuits that have been filed against someone in your profession for negligence? __ Yes __ No

8. Is your annual combined household income greater than $40,000 per year? __ Yes __ No

9. Do you routinely keep more than $10,000 in your checking, savings and/or money market accounts? __ Yes __ No

10. Do you have children or any employees or independent contractors supervised directly by you? __ Yes __ No

Scoring: Look over your answers to the quiz. If you answered yes to more than five of the questions, then chances are you should have some form of asset protection plan to protect you and your wealth from creditor claims.

Chapter Two

Keeping It Legal

In the last chapter we briefly discussed the fact that you cannot use asset protection planning for protecting against lawsuits that have already been filed or threatened against you. If you can't use asset protection to escape from existing debts that you legitimately created, what can you use it to accomplish?

Asset protection can be properly and legally used to avoid the claims of creditors that you do not already know about and whose claims you could not reasonably anticipate considering your present circumstances. These unknowns are the creditors from whom you legally can protect your assets, and there is absolutely nothing immoral, illegal, or improper about using asset protection planning for that purpose.

Don't Abuse Your Asset Protection Plan

If you abuse your asset protection plan by using it for improper purposes, there's a good chance that a court will set the plan aside. Even if you created an absolutely bullet-proof plan that the court doesn't have the power or jurisdiction to set aside, you may find yourself in jail for contempt if you ignore or refuse to abide by a court order to use the control you have over your asset protection plan to make your assets available to satisfy your obligations. This is a dangerous game to play and one to be avoided.

If you abuse your asset protection plan by using it for improper purposes, there's a good chance that a court will set the plan aside.

How Much of Your Wealth Can You Legally Protect?

Chances are, if you don't have any existing obligations or debts, then you can protect most of your assets by placing them into an asset protection plan. Unfortunately, almost all of us have one or more debts or obligations to deal with. As a general rule of thumb, you should leave enough assets outside of your asset protection plan to cover both your current and reasonably foreseeable debts and expenses.

The best way to determine how much of your property you can protect is to prepare a personal financial statement to determine your net worth. To do so, simply list all of your assets and all of your liabilities and then subtract the liabilities from the assets. The result is your net worth. If you don't already have a personal financial statement, you can use a format similar to the one provided at the end of this section.

Once you have determined your net worth, the first step is to prepare a list of foreseeable debt. Think about any debts you are about to incur or might reasonably expect to incur in the foreseeable future. For example, if you are in business for yourself and you are about to sign a new lease for office space, you should include the value of the lease on your foreseeable debts list. If you are about to buy a new car, house, boat, or some other major asset, or plan to within the next year, then your list should also include any debt you will incur in connection with the purchase. Once you've completed your list of foreseeable debts, add them together, and subtract the total from your net worth. The resulting number equals your potentially protectable assets.

The second step in determining how much of your property you can protect is to look at your income and expenses. You should not try to protect more of your income producing assets than you need to pay your debts as they become due. For example, let's assume that your home mortgage payment and other monthly debt service payments total $2,000 per month. Also assume that your net take-home pay after taxes is $1,800 per month, and you have savings and investments that provide another $1,000 per month. In this example, your net earnings from all sources is $2,800 and your total monthly debt service is $2,000. Subtracting the debt service from your net income leaves $800 of extra income. That means that you could protect the savings and investment assets that provide that extra $800.

To reconcile the first step with the second, determine whether you need any of the potentially protectable assets that you identified in the first step to meet your monthly debt service as determined in the second step. If you do, then those assets should not be removed from the assets available to your creditors. If you don't need any or all of these assets to meet your debt service, then the unneeded portion can be completely protected, and any creditor challenging the transfer will probably fail in any attempt to get to them to satisfy any claims against you. By using this test, you can determine your total protectable assets under both of the criteria that creditors and courts most frequently use to determine whether you have crossed the line between permissible asset protection planning and fraudulent asset transfers.

Form 1
Financial Statement Form

Description	Asset	Liability
Cash in Bank		
Certificates of Deposit		
Money Market Accounts		
Stocks, Bonds, and Mutual Funds		
Money People Owe You		
Home		
Business		
Other Real Estate		
Retirement Accounts		
Cash Value Life Insurance Policies		
Cars		
Jewelry		
Household Furnishings		
Boats, Planes, Patents, Copyrights, and Other Miscellaneous Property		
Money You Owe Other People		
Mortgage (or Total Remaining Rent Due Under Real Property Leases)		
Loans On Cars		
Credit Card Debts		
Leases, Loans Against Life Insurance Policies and Other Miscellaneous Debts		
Totals		
Net Worth = Total Assets - Total Liabilities		

Form 2
Foreseeable Debts

Description	Worth	Debt
New Cars		
New Home		
Student Loans		
Anticipated Medical Expenses		
Other		
Totals		
Protectable Assets = Net Worth - Foreseeable Debts		

Potential Creditors v. Future Creditors

In cases regarding asset protection, the law makes a distinction between potential creditors and future creditors. The difference between these two types of creditors is not completely clear, and different courts have approached it in different ways. However, a general rule of thumb is that potential creditors are those that you do not yet owe any money, but to whom it is reasonably foreseeable that you will or could owe money in the future. Future creditors, on the other hand, are those you do not currently owe anything, and to whom it is not reasonably foreseeable that you will or could owe anything in the foreseeable future.

For example, if you are a building contractor who builds and sells residential homes, a potential creditor would be someone to whom you sold a house that you knew was defective or who had complained about the house and threatened to sue you if the problems weren't fixed. Based on these facts and circumstances, it is reasonably foreseeable that this person could become a creditor if you fail to fix the defects. A future creditor would be someone you do not yet know who purchases a house that you build two years from now.

You will probably be able to protect your current assets from claims made by the second person, but not the first. Use this distinction between potential and future creditors as a guide when determining the amount of assets you can legitimately expect to protect.

Fraudulent Transfers Acts

Many people believe that if they get sued, they can simply put everything in their spouse's name or that of a family member or friend to protect the assets from creditors' claims. This belief is simply not true. Creditor protection laws based on the Uniform Fraudulent Transfers Act have been enacted in most states to prevent debtors from taking steps with the intent to defraud, hinder, or delay legitimate creditors from being able to move against a debtor's assets to satisfy the creditors' claims. If a debtor attempts to transfer assets and the transfer violates the applicable statutes, then civil and criminal penalties may apply, in addition to a right for the creditors to "unwind" the transfers and recover the assets to satisfy their claims.

Badges of Fraud

Because it is impossible for the court to climb inside your head at the time you transferred assets to determine exactly what you were thinking when you made the transfers, general rules of thumb were developed to assist the court in determining whether you had the requisite intent to defraud, delay, or hinder a creditor at the time an asset transfer was made. These rules of thumb are called "badges of fraud," and they can create a presumption that you transferred assets with the intent necessary to permit the court to unwind those transfers under the fraudulent transfers laws.

Keep in mind that just because a creditor can establish the existence of one or more badges of fraud, that doesn't necessarily mean that what you did was fraudulent. It also doesn't mean that the creditor will succeed in overturning your asset transfers under the Uniform Fraudulent Transfers Act.

All a badge of fraud means is that the creditor has provided evidence from which an inference of fraudulent intent may be made. You would be wise to attempt to prove that despite the presence of the badge(s) of fraud, you did not intend to make a fraudulent transfer. Unless the creditor can convince the court or jury that you did have fraudulent intent when you made the transfer, chances are that the creditor will lose and the transfer will be allowed to stand untouched by the court.

There are several badges of fraud, the most common of which are described in Table 2.

If any of the badges of fraud are present in your situation, then you probably should reconsider whether you can do any meaningful asset protection planning until they are eliminated. Remember, you can get not only yourself, but also your family and friends in trouble by transferring assets in violation of the creditor protection laws that have been enacted in your state.

Table 2
Badges of Fraud

Badge	Example
Whether the transfer was to an "insider" such as a friend, family member, professional advisor or business associate.	You are sued for a personal injury accident and you transfer all of your assets to your brother-in-law.
Whether you continued to possess or control the property that was transferred even after the date that it was transferred.	You sign away all of your interest in your car to a third party, but you continue to drive and use the car even after the transfer.
Whether the transfer was disclosed or concealed.	You get a home equity loan from your parents and give them a first deed of trust on your home, but the deed of trust is never recorded at the county recorder's office.
Whether the transfer was of substantially all of your assets.	You transfer your home, cars, investments, and business assets and leave yourself with little or no assets to meet your debts and obligations.
Whether you left the state or country or otherwise tried to run away from your obligations.	You transfer all of your assets to a third party who lives in the Cayman Islands, and then leave the country yourself.

Table 2 cont.

Badge	Example
Whether you removed or concealed assets from your creditors.	You lease a retail store space in a mall, but when business is bad you can't pay the rent so you make a "midnight move" and leave the store, taking all of the assets, even though there are still four years remaining on your lease.
Whether the money or property you received for the assets that you transferred was roughly the same as the assets transferred.	You sell your completely paid-for home, which would appraise for $225,000, to a third party for $100,000.
Whether you made the transfer shortly before or after a substantial debt was incurred.	You plan to enter into a lease for a commercial office space, and shortly before or after signing the lease, you transfer all of your assets to a corporation owned by your spouse.
Whether you transferred the essential assets of your business to another creditor who then transferred them to a person closely related to you.	You get sued for slander. Fearing a loss of the lawsuit, you grant an unrelated person a lien on all of your business assets, but that person then transfers the lien in a side deal to your daughter.
Whether before the transfer was made a creditor sued or threatened to sue you.	A business acquaintance tips you off to a lawsuit that is about to be filed against you by a disgruntled former employee. You then transfer all of your assets to your parents.

Bankruptcy Laws

While this book is about asset protection planning and not bankruptcy, the two overlap to some degree. Federal law provides the bankruptcy trustee with a great deal of power to ferret out and seize a debtor's assets and unwind transactions which the trustee deems inappropriate or unfair to creditors.

For purposes of this book, you should know that a bankruptcy trustee generally has the power to unwind any transfers: 1) to an unrelated person or creditor within the ninety days immediately before the filing of the bankruptcy petition, and 2) to any person who is an "insider" of the debtor within one year prior to the filing of the bankruptcy petition. This power is known as the "voidable preference transfer" and is granted to the trustee to prevent debtors from preferring one creditor over another.

Federal law provides the bankruptcy trustee with a great deal of power to ferret out and seize a debtor's assets and unwind transactions which the trustee deems inappropriate or unfair to creditors.

A second bankruptcy power vested in the trustee is the "fraudulent conveyance power." This power permits the trustee to set aside as fraudulent, transfers for less than fair and adequate consideration within the statutory period. For all intents and purposes, this power is seldom used to set aside transfers for less than fair and adequate considerations where those transfers occurred more than two years before the filing of the bankruptcy petition.

Keep these laws in mind if you are contemplating the possibility of filing bankruptcy within two years of making any transfers to your asset protection plan. If you make the transfers and are then unable to unwind them on the trustee's order, you may find that the bankruptcy court will deny your request to discharge all of your former debts.

Money Laundering, Technology Transfer, and Boycott Laws

State and federal laws related to money laundering, sensitive technology transfers, or boycott laws can affect your asset protection planning if they apply to you.

Money Laundering Laws

Money laundering laws are designed to keep people who have cash or other assets generated from illegal or improper activities from taking steps to give the appearance that those assets were generated from legitimate activities.

Technology Transfer Laws

Technology transfer laws are designed to keep sensitive technological information from leaving the country and/or falling into the hands of unfriendly governments or groups who might then use that technology against the United States or its allies for an improper purpose.

Boycott Laws

To show its contempt for certain governmental activities of foreign countries, the United States from time to time enacts boycotts preventing the importation or exportation of goods and/or services to and from countries conducting such activities.

If any of the asset transfers that you contemplate in connection with your asset protection plan will involve money laundering laws, technology transfer laws, or boycott laws, you should consult an attorney or the Secretary of State's office in your state to determine whether those transfers are permissible.

Federal Tax and Other Reporting Obligations

Depending on the transfers that you make in connection with your asset protection plan and the number and types of entities formed in connection with the plan, you may have to file one or more forms with the Internal Revenue Service and other government entities. Table 3 illustrates several potential forms and filings that may need to be made depending on your particular plan.

Table 3
Major Reporting Requirements for Asset Protection Plans

Form	Description/When Needed
IRS Form 1120	Annual corporate tax return.
IRS Form 1120-S	Annual return for a subchapter S corporation.
IRS Form 1065	Annual return for a partnership.
IRS Form 1041	Annual return for a trust.
IRS Form 3520	Creation of, or transfers to, certain foreign trusts. Must be filed on or before the 90th day after the creation of, or transfer of, any money to a foreign trust. Filed with Philadelphia Internal Revenue Service Center. Information required includes name of trust, date formed, date of property transfer, trust termination date, income distribution requirements, trustee name and address, and grantor and beneficiary information.
IRS Form 926	Return by a United States transferor of property to a foreign corporation, foreign estate or trust, or foreign partnership. Must be filed each time assets are transferred to a foreign trust, usually on the day of the transfer. Filed at Internal Revenue Service Center where person who created the trust files personal tax return. Requires grantor, beneficiary, and trustee information, and information about assets transferred. Used to determine whether §1491 excise tax is due as a result of the transfer.
IRS Form 709	United States estate, gift, and generation skipping transfer tax return. Reports gift transfers to asset protection plan entities and beneficiaries. Generally due at same time and filed with same service center as the income tax return of the person creating the asset protection plan.
IRS Form 1040	The form that you know and love, where all income reportable to you from your asset protection plan must be reported annually.
IRS Form 5471	Information return of United States persons with respect to certain foreign corporations or foreign partnerships. Must be filed by United States citizens or residents who acquire 5% or more interest in a foreign corporation disclosing that ownership. Filed with your personal income tax return.
IRS Form 3520-A	Annual return of a foreign trust with United States beneficiaries. Filed by persons who create foreign trusts that have United States beneficiaries. Due on 15th day of fourth month following end of that person's tax year.

Table 3 cont.

Form	Description/When Needed
Treasury Department Form F 90-22.1 (no longer used, but a successor form may be required at a later date)	Reporting form formerly required to be filed by any United States citizen with custody, control, or signature power over a foreign bank account. Disclosure is also required on your United States tax return.
IRS Form 56	Notice concerning fiduciary relationship filed by the trustee of an asset protection trust with the first trust tax return in the year that the trust is created.
IRS Form 4790 (no longer used but a successor form may be required at a later date).	Form formerly required to report international transportation of currency or monetary bearer instruments by anyone physically transferring, mailing, or shipping cash or bearer securities in the aggregate amount of $10,000 or more outside the United States. Filed with United States Customs Service.
IRS Form 8300	Report of cash payments over $10,000 which must be filed by any person who receives more than $10,000 in cash or foreign currency in the course of their trade or business.
IRS Form 4789	Currency transaction report filed by banks where transactions in cash or monetary instruments are $10,000 or more.
Bank Deposit Account Records	Banks are required to maintain deposit account records showing each transaction and all checks issued by the bank in excess of $100 for five years, and banks must make these records available to inquiring government agencies.
SEC Form 13-D	A form which must be filed by beneficial owners of 5% or more of the securities of a publicly-held company. It discloses ownership and owner information.
SEC Form 3	A form which must be filed with the SEC by beneficial owners of 10% or more of the securities of a publicly held company, as well as certain control persons.

Ten Tips for Making Asset Transfers to Your Asset Protection Plan

Tip 1	Don't make any asset transfers after you have been sued or after a lawsuit has been threatened, either verbally or in writing.
Tip 2	Don't transfer all of your assets at the same time. Be sure that you leave enough assets in your name to meet your existing and reasonably anticipated obligations as they come due.
Tip 3	Create public records that do not indicate transfers to insiders by avoiding transfers to people with the same last name as yours.
Tip 4	Develop ideas and a paper trail that indicates that the primary purpose for any transfers was motivated by business, moral, tax, or estate planning concerns, not asset protection.
Tip 5	Don't make transfers to people who don't believe in the legitimacy of your asset protection plan or who aren't willing to stand firm if your transfers are challenged.
Tip 6	Make transfers over time and to more than one type of asset protection entity to spread your risk in the event that a creditor succeeds in avoiding part of your asset protection plan.
Tip 7	Obtain independent appraisals of the property that you transfer into your asset protection plan so that you will be able to defend the values if they are challenged by creditors.
Tip 8	Make full disclosure of any transfers by recording deeds with the county recorder, filing UCC-1's at the Secretary of State's office, and publishing other transfers in your local newspaper. If you make these disclosures voluntarily, they will provide strong evidence that you did not intend to hide anything from your creditors.
Tip 9	Don't take actions that are inconsistent with the transfers that you make. If you transfer an asset but continue to retain possession, you provide creditors with a strategy to attack the transfer and set it aside.
Tip 10	Don't limit yourself to one asset protection strategy. If you can mortgage an asset, transfer it to a family limited partnership, and then sell it to an asset protection trust, that will provide more protection than doing only one of these things.

Quick Quiz—Can You Qualify for Asset Protection Planning?

1. Are you the plaintiff or defendant in a lawsuit at this time? __ Yes __ No

2. Has anyone threatened to sue you within the past year either verbally or in writing? __ Yes __ No

3. Are your liabilities higher than your assets? __ Yes __ No

4. Are you planning on entering into any major transactions that would result in a large amount of debt? __ Yes __ No

5. Considering your reasonably foreseeable obligations, do your assets minus liabilities minus those foreseeable obligations amount to a negative number? __ Yes __ No

6. Are you willing to comply with federal and state reporting requirements in connection with the implementation of your asset protection plan? __ Yes __ No

7. Are you willing to continue to comply with the annual reporting requirements that apply to your asset protection plan? __ Yes __ No

8. Do any of the assets that you want to protect come from illegal or questionable activities such as gambling? __ Yes __ No

9. Are any of the assets that you would be transferring into your asset protection plan related to defense, aerospace, or technology so that they may be subject to restrictions on transfers? __ Yes __ No

10. Are any of the assets that you would be transferring into your asset protection plan located in or would they be transferred to a country that is subject to a boycott or other sanctions by the United States government? __ Yes __ No

Scoring: If you answered yes to any of the ten questions above, then there may be one or more limitations on your ability to enter into an asset protection plan.

Chapter Three

Dealing with Creditors

Anyone who has ever had a dispute with a creditor knows how frustrating it can be to try to resolve the dispute. Most creditors are reluctant to accept less than the value of the debt to satisfy it, and they usually aren't very receptive to the idea of working out a payment plan, even if it means they will get the full amount of their claim. This chapter discusses how to deal with creditors when you don't have the ability to pay and how to use your asset protection plan to your advantage in negotiating favorable settlements and payment plans.

The creditors who are discussed in this chapter can be your normal creditors to whom you owe debts for credit cards and instant loan purchases, mortgage lenders, and consumer credit agencies, or they can be judgment creditors who have obtained their creditor status by suing you and winning a judgment in the context of a contested court action. Either way, if you can't pay these creditors everything that you owe them when payment is due, they are likely to come looking to see what they can get from you without your cooperation. If you know how to face this unpleasant situation, you have a much better chance of coming out of it with an acceptable result and hopefully some assets as well.

Settling Disputes with Creditors

Asset protection can't stop people from suing you. Anyone can sue anyone else at any time for any reason, but a properly designed and implemented asset protection plan can provide strong incentives for creditors to settle their claims against you on favorable terms.

When a creditor or potential plaintiff first approaches you about a claim, don't refuse to talk with them. Learn all that you can about their claim to determine whether you think you have any exposure. If you think you do, then find out what they want. Tell them you feel you shouldn't have to pay their claim, but you are interested in doing what's fair, so you're willing to give them something less than what they want in order to settle the claim without the financial and emotional costs of litigation. Explain to them that litigation is usually an all or nothing affair, with the loser left unsatisfied and possibly paying the winner's costs and attorneys' fees. Say that you would prefer to settle and put the whole dispute behind you.

Get It in Writing

If the creditor is willing to settle, don't trust your memory and a canceled check to document the agreement. Prepare a settlement agreement that fully explains that your agreement with the creditor is to settle all claims either of you may have against the other based on any prior dealings. Some states require the inclusion of special language in settlement agreements to completely protect the parties. Check your state's laws to see if this applies to your situation. There are several important points to include in your settlement agreement; Table 4 provides several suggestions for clauses that you may want to use.

Just because you aren't successful in settling a dispute before it goes to litigation doesn't mean that you can't settle it after your creditor has gone to court and obtained a judgment against you. Most of the really large jury verdicts you hear about in the media are settled for much less after the judgment is rendered. There are many incentives for a creditor to settle their claim for less than the full amount, even after a judgment is rendered. First, you might choose to appeal the judgment, and even if you didn't win the appeal, it would take more attorneys' fees, more costs, and more time for the judgment creditor to see any money on the claim.

Additionally, anyone who has ever obtained a judgment against someone else knows there's a big difference between getting the judgment and getting paid. A large judgment is practically worthless if the debtor has no assets to satisfy it, and after you have completed your asset protection planning, you will have very few non-exempt assets for a judgment creditor to seize to satisfy their judgment. Faced with the prospect of additional litigation to locate your assets and overturn your asset protection plan, with no certainty of success, the judg-

...there's a big difference between getting the judgment and getting paid.

ment creditor will likely be in a very favorable mood for settlement. At that point, you can offer to settle the claim for much less than the amount of the judgment and sign a written settlement and release agreement saying the claim has been satisfied in full.

Table 4
Sample Clauses for Settlement Agreements with Creditors

Clause	Example
Consideration Clause	In consideration of the mutual covenants, representations, and releases contained herein, and in exchange for other good and valuable consideration, the adequacy, sufficiency, and receipt of which is hereby acknowledged, the parties hereby agree as follows:
No Admission Clause	Neither party to this Agreement acknowledges or admits any wrongdoing in connection with the subject matter of this Agreement.
No Additional Consideration Clause	No other funds shall be required to be paid from [you] to [your creditor] or from [your creditor] to [you].
Non-disparagement Clause	Both parties agree to refrain from making any disparaging remarks about the other party to any third party for a period of one year following the execution of this agreement.
Release of Claims	[you] and [your creditor], for themselves and their respective directors, officers, employees, shareholders, spouses, attorneys, principals, agents, successors, assignors, parent organizations, subsidiaries, affiliates, heirs, executors, administrators, and assigns, if any, (the "Released Parties") hereby mutually release, remise, and forever discharge the Released Parties, and all other persons and entities, whether individual, corporate, or otherwise, who are or may become liable in any fashion for any or all liabilities or claims arising from or related to the Disputes, or the negotiation, execution, performance, or termination of any agreements relating to the Disputes, or claims which were or could have been set forth or asserted of and from any and all claims, judgments, demands, causes of action, suits, actions, controversies, counterclaims, third-party actions, proceedings, or liabilities of any kind or nature whatsoever, without exception, known or unknown, accrued or unaccrued, whether in law or in equity, and whether in contract, warranty, tort, or otherwise, which either, jointly or severally, ever had, now has, or may have, claim, allege, or assert, relating to or arising from the Disputes, the negotiation, execution, performance or termination of any agreements relating to the Disputes, or any claims, demands, and allegations, which have been or could have been set forth and asserted in any litigation.
Covenant Not to Sue	Both parties agree to refrain from instituting any suit against any of the Released Parties relating to the subject matter of this Agreement.

Table 4 cont.

Clause	Example
After Discovered Facts Clause	Each party to this agreement acknowledges and is aware that they may hereafter discover facts different from or in addition to the facts which they now know or believe to be true with respect to the subject matter of this Agreement, but it is their intention to fully and finally release each other from any and all manner of liabilities and claims as described in this Agreement which exist or may exist, regardless of any such facts.
Entire Agreement Clause	This Agreement reflects the final expression of the parties' agreement and contains a complete and exclusive statement of the terms of that Agreement, which terms supersede all previous verbal and written agreements.
Zipper Clause	No part of this Agreement may be amended or modified in any way unless such amendment or modification is expressed in a writing signed by all parties to this Agreement.
Severability Clause	If any provision of this Agreement is held by a court to be unenforceable or invalid for any reason, the remaining provisions of this Agreement shall be unaffected by such holding. If the invalidation of any such provision materially alters the agreement of the parties, then the parties shall immediately adopt new provisions to replace those which were declared invalid.

In addition to the clauses presented above, there may be other clauses that you will want to insert into your settlement agreement.

If you cannot successfully negotiate a favorable settlement with a creditor, you may have to endure a debtor's examination. A debtor's examination is a legal procedure permitting a creditor to ask questions about the nature and location of your assets to assist in collecting a debt. Prior to the creditor asking you these questions, you are placed under oath, and if you lie about your assets, you do so under penalty of perjury. If you anticipate the possibility of undergoing a debtor's exam as you design and implement your asset protection plan, you can place yourself in a position where you neither have to lie nor reveal all of your asset protection secrets to a probing creditor. To assist you in anticipating the kinds of questions a creditor might ask you in a debtor's exam, consider the questions in Table 5.

The questions listed provide an indication of just some of the issues you can expect to be asked about in a debtor's exam. A skilled creditor or examining attorney will ask many, many more questions in much greater detail. Knowing these types of questions will be asked, think about how to structure your asset transfers, asset and entity ownership, and overall asset protection plan to anticipate these questions and provide plausible answers in the face of a debtor's examination.

Table 5
Possible Questions Asked in a Debtor's Examination

Subject	Possible Questions
Employment Questions	Are you currently employed as a full or part-time employee, and if so, by whom and at what salary?
Sources of Income	Please describe all sources of your income, including business income, salaries, consulting and independent contractor fees, dividends, interest income, gifts from others, trusts, etc., and the names and addresses of the payors.
Affiliations	Please list the names and addresses of all corporations, partnerships, limited liability companies, trusts, and other entities in which you are an officer, director, shareholder, partner, trustor, trustee, beneficiary, member, manager, or with which you are otherwise affiliated.
Cash and Cash Equivalent Assets	Please list the names, addresses, account names, and account numbers of all bank, certificate of deposit, money market, savings, and related accounts over which you have or have had signature authority in the past five years.
Stocks, Bonds, and Investment Securities	Please list the names, addresses, account names, and account numbers of all securities brokerage accounts, stocks, bonds, and other securities that you have controlled or owned in the past five years.
Bank Records	Please provide copies of all bank deposits and disbursements made by you or your spouse for the past five years, along with copies of deposit receipts and check registers indicating the source of funds.
Hard Assets	Please list the names and addresses of any storage facilities, warehouses, mini-warehouses, mini-storage units, safe deposit boxes, and safes that you have, maintain, or have access or control over, and provide a complete list of the contents of each.
Bearer Securities	Please describe the names and addresses of any corporations with bearer shares whose shares, securities, or certificates representing an ownership interest have at any time been in your possession, whether for your own account or that of someone else.
Cars	Please describe any cars that you or your spouse own, lease, or otherwise possess, control, or use, and the names and addresses of the registered owners thereof.
Boats	Same question as above, but with respect to boats.
Planes	Same question as above, but with respect to planes.
Jewelry	Please describe any jewelry that you or your spouse own, lease, or otherwise possess, control, or use, and the names and addresses of the owners thereof.

Table 5 cont.

Subject	Possible Questions
Collections	Please describe any collections, that you or your spouse own, lease, or otherwise possess, control, or use, and the names and addresses of the owners thereof. Examples include, coin, stamp, gun, musical instrument, plates, artwork, book, doll, toy, computer, recorded music, car, train, and other collections.
Antiques and Other Valuables	Please describe any household furnishings or other functional assets that are of greater value than that of typical assets that could replace those assets and perform the same function despite their lower value that you or your spouse own, lease, or otherwise possess, control, or use, and the names and addresses of the owners thereof.
Other Assets	Please describe any real property, insurance policies, or other assets of whatever type that you or your spouse own, lease or otherwise possess, control, or use, and the names and addresses of the owners thereof.
Spouse's Assets	Same questions as above, but with respect to your spouse.

Chapter Four

How to Protect Your Home with Little or No Effort

One of the most important assets you will ever own is your home. It provides security, not just from the elements, but an emotional, peace-of-mind security that can only come from owning the place in which you live. Even if you don't have much equity in your home, or if you don't have many assets other than your home equity, you should consider taking advantage of state and federal laws enacted to allow you to have a place to live no matter how bad things get with your creditors. Depending on which state you live in, you may already be protected, but many states require a filing at the county recorder's office for the county you live in to take advantage of statutory homestead exemptions.

Homestead Laws Are Based on Sound Public Policy

Homestead laws have been enacted in many states to promote a public policy of allowing people the security of knowing at least some portion of their home ownership will always be safe from creditors, unless the homeowner debtor specifically grants a creditor a lien on his or her home.

Why Many People Don't Take Advantage of Homestead Protection

Many people have no idea that homestead protection is available to them. Others aren't sure if they can qualify or are afraid that their mortgage lender won't like it if they file a homestead exemption. Still other people simply never take the time to take the steps necessary to obtain homestead protection. Whatever the case, there is simply no good reason for failing to secure your home with a homestead.

...there is simply no good reason for failing to secure your home with a homestead.

Where to Look to Learn More about Homesteads

You should check the laws of your state to determine whether a homestead is available and, if so, what steps you should take to maximize its protection. If you decide to do this research yourself, the best place to start is with a call to your county recorder's office. They should be able to tell you if a homestead is available. If that doesn't work, try calling the county tax assessor's office to see if they can provide any guidance. If all else fails, try doing the research yourself at a law library or consulting an attorney, real estate broker, or financial planner. Eventually, you should be able to find someone who can tell you whether and to what extent homestead protection is available.

State laws vary widely as to how much home equity can be protected by a homestead exemption. For example, a married couple in California typically receives a $75,000 homestead, although that amount can increase to as much as $100,000 for blind or disabled couples over age 65.

Nevada and Arizona provide homesteads as well, and in Arizona, no filing is necessary for such homestead protection; however, Texas and Florida offer homeowners the best homestead protection. Texas exempts anything built on up to 1 acre in the city and up to 200 acres in rural areas, while Florida provides the same protection on areas of up to 1/2 acre and 160 acres, respectively.

California also provides additional homestead protection for those who sell their home by protecting the proceeds from the sale for up to six months while the homeowner attempts to locate a new home in which to reinvest and re-homestead his or her equity. However, this protection is only available if you record a declaration of homestead at the county recorder's office for the county in which the home is located. Your state may have its own peculiarities, and you should check the law to determine whether filing a declaration affords you any additional asset protection.

Homesteads Protect Your Principal Residence

Keep in mind that homesteads generally only apply to real estate that you own and use as your principle residence. Usually no protection is provided for residential rental real estate or commercial properties. Some states restrict your ability to homestead condominiums and cooperatives, apartments located in a multiple dwelling structure, or mobile homes. Also, be sure to check your state's homestead laws to determine if it is possible to lose your homestead protection under certain circumstances. For example, when you sell your home, don't assume the declaration of homestead that you filed on your previous home automatically carries over to your new home.

Ten Steps for Getting the Most out of Your State's Homestead Laws

Step 1	Determine whether the state you live in offers any homestead protection. If you aren't sure, ask your county recorder, county tax assessor, real estate broker, attorney, or financial planner.
Step 2	Find out if there are any restrictions on the types of property your state's homestead laws protect to see if your home is protected.
Step 3	If your current home does not qualify for protection under these laws, consider selling it and buying one that does.
Step 4	Determine whether you need to take any steps to obtain homestead protection by filing any documents with any government agencies or public offices. For example, you may need to file a declaration of homestead to get homestead protection.
Step 5	Determine the maximum amount of home equity protected by your state's laws. If you have money in other assets that don't have similar protection, consider shifting that money into your home equity, up to the full amount of the homestead exemption. Even if you exceed the exemption by a small amount, most creditors won't pursue your home, because they know that costs and administrative fees will consume several thousand dollars of the available equity.
Step 6	If the value of your home less all existing mortgages and the homestead exemption is greater than $5,000, consider granting a second mortgage to a trusted friend or a relative with a different last name from yours.
Step 7	Determine whether your state's homestead laws do not protect your home equity from certain kinds of debts or debts that were incurred at a certain point in time.
Step 8	If, after completing Step Seven above, you find that some debts are not protected by your homestead, work to pay off those debts before retiring exempted debts.
Step 9	Before selling your home, determine whether your new home qualifies for homestead protection, what steps you must take to protect the new home and whether the proceeds from the sale of your current home will be protected.
Step 10	If your state does not provide adequate homestead protection and your creditors are in hot pursuit, consider relocating to a state such as Texas or Florida where homesteads are much more generous than in other states.

Relocation May Be the Answer

If your state doesn't offer the homestead protection that you need and you are under an intense attack from your creditors, consider relocating to a state with favorable homestead laws and investing your money into a home there. However, don't make the mistake that some make by moving to one of these homestead favored states and immediately thumbing your nose at your creditors by filing bankruptcy. This has happened to some very famous people who moved, invested in multi-million dollar homes, and then filed bankruptcy. Sensing the inequity of allowing these people to escape their responsibilities to creditors, the courts disallowed bankruptcy discharges. The best bet, if you need to pursue the relocation strategy, is to relocate, homestead, and then wait a couple of years before filing for bankruptcy. The preceding table provides an action guide for getting the most out of your state's homestead laws.

Retirement Funds

The United States Supreme Court has held that all Employee Retirement Income Security Act (ERISA) qualified plans are exempt from creditors other than the IRS; however, it did not provide a clear indication of which plans were ERISA qualified plans. Public retirement plans have always been exempt, but the fate of private plans was uncertain until only recently. Corporate pension, profit sharing, money purchase, 401(k), defined benefit, and ESOP plans are exempt, but IRA accounts and Keoghs exempt status may depend on your state's laws. You may only be entitled to an exemption to the extent the funds are necessary to provide for the support of yourself, your spouse, and your dependents when you retire.

Insurance Exemptions

Life insurance exemptions are generally provided by all states, and your state may offer any of the following benefits depending on state law:

- exemption from attachment by creditors of policy holder
- exemption from attachment by creditors of beneficiaries
- dollar limitations on the amount of the exemption
- exemption of cash value of policies
- exemption of proceeds from insurance policies

Annuity Exemptions

Many states that provide insurance exemptions also provide exemptions for annuities. For example, Florida exempts annuities without any limitation on value.

Chapter Five

Using Partnerships to Protect Your Personal Assets

Considering how difficult it is to save money and accumulate wealth in today's ever-changing economic climate, it makes sense to take the necessary steps to assure that no one can take away the things for which you have worked so hard. Wouldn't it be nice to know that no matter how bad things get, no one can take away your personal assets unless you give them the power to by pledging them as collateral for a loan?

This chapter will tell you how to take the necessary steps to place your personal assets into a structure that will keep them safe from creditors who seek to recover a claim against them. By placing your personal assets into a partnership with your family members, you can generally protect those assets from any claim by any creditor other than a spouse. In fact, unless you grant a creditor a security interest in those assets, it will be virtually impossible for anyone to succeed in taking them away from you.

So what's so special about partnerships? Why does holding your assets in a partnership provide any more protection than owning them outright or in a corporation? The reason is simple. Special laws apply to any creditor who gets a judgment against someone who owns an interest in a partnership. These laws provide that a creditor of one partner can't seize partnership assets to satisfy a claim against only that partner. Instead, the creditor must get a "charging order" against that partner's interest in the partnership. This is the creditors only effective remedy, unless a claim can be made against all of the partners of the partnership.

Charging Orders

A charging order is similar to another type of order creditors sometimes get to satisfy a judgment against someone—a "wage garnishment order." Both of these orders permit a creditor to serve notice on a third party, letting them know that the creditor has a claim against the debtor and requiring any payment be made directly to the creditor. A creditor who gets a judgment against a partner of a partnership must generally get a charging order and serve it on the partnership. The partnership must then make any payments or distributions of partnership property that would have otherwise been made directly to the partner directly to the creditor instead.

As you can see, this provides some great asset protection planning opportunities. If you place your house and cars into a partnership with other family members, a creditor of any single family member will be prevented from seizing and selling those assets to satisfy a claim. Instead, the creditor will have to get a charging order, demanding the partnership pay any wages or property distributions it makes to the partner, against whom the creditor has the judgment, directly to the creditor until the creditor's claim is satisfied. The beauty of the charging order is that chances are good the partnership will never make a distribution to the family member with the creditor problem, so the creditor's claim may never be satisfied.

Foreclosure Actions by Creditors

Some courts have held that a creditor can move to foreclose on the partner's interest in the partnership if the creditor's claim cannot be satisfied within a reasonable amount of time. However, even if the creditor is permitted to foreclose the interest, the creditor does not automatically become a partner in the partnership. Instead, the creditor simply becomes an owner of the former partner's interest in the partnership, with no right to vote in partnership business, demand payments or property distributions, or if the partnership agreement is drafted properly, cause a dissolution of the partnership.

In fact, there is at least one very good reason for a creditor not to foreclose on a partnership interest in a family held partnership; if the creditor becomes a partner, then the creditor must pay income taxes on its share of partnership income, even if the partnership makes no payments or distributions to the creditor. The partnership taxation rules in the Internal Revenue Code provide that partners must pay income taxes on their share of partnership income whether or not they receive any distributions or payments. That means the creditor could end up owning an interest in a partnership that would be difficult to sell because the family assets produce little if any income. Further, the creditor would be stuck paying income taxes on the income it never received because the remaining family member partners would never declare a distribution, knowing that the creditor would receive a portion of it.

The Partnership Strategy Encourages Favorable Settlements

Faced with the unappealing prospects of holding a charging order that would never satisfy its claim against the debtor partner, or foreclosing on the partner's interest and owning and paying taxes on an interest that could probably never be sold and will never yield income, the creditor would be very likely to consider an offer to settle the debtor partner's debt on favorable terms. In this way, each family member is positioned for maximum protection, because no creditor can attach the family's assets unless the other family member partners consent. Most creditor's will either not pursue their claim beyond a charging order or will agree to accept favorable terms for settling their claims by accepting an amount significantly less than the amount of their claims or by agreeing to an installment payment plan for satisfaction of the debt, or both.

Using Family Limited Partnerships

While general partnerships have many significant advantages, they also have some disadvantages that are important to consider. Most general partnerships are an all-for-one-and-one-for-all affair. That is, general partnerships usually permit all partners to vote on partnership business. While this arrangement works well in many business partnerships, it may not necessarily be the best way to operate with respect to your family assets. One alternative to the general partnership is the family limited partnership.

A family limited partnership is similar to the general partnership in many respects. It offers all of the creditor protection advantages discussed above, but it also provides some additional benefits. In a limited partnership, there are one or more general partners who run the partnership and one or more limited partners who have an ownership interest in the partnership, but have little say in the day-to-day operations of the partnership. The general partners are personally liable for partnership debts; however, the limited partners' liability is limited to their investment, if any, in the limited partnership. General partners may be corporations if their lack of limited liability becomes an issue.

The chief advantage of a family limited partnership over a family general partnership is that whoever is creating and contributing the majority of the assets to the limited partnership can designate themselves as the general partner, while those who are contributing few if any assets to the limited partnership can be designated as limited partners. In this way, whoever creates the limited partnership and contributes the most assets to it can remain in complete control of those assets without worrying about the other partners. Generally, in the family limited partnership, parents will create the limited partnership, designate themselves as general partners, and contribute the family home, cars, and similar assets, while the children will contribute no assets and are designated as limited partners.

The ownership of family limited partnership interests is usually structured so that only a very small proportion of the partnership is owned by the general partners, with the bulk of the family limited partnership owned by the limited partners. For tax reasons beyond the scope of this discussion, the general partners usually own 2 percent of the family limited partnership, with the limited partners owning the remaining 98 percent.

Using a Trust with a Family Limited Partnership

Of the 98 percent limited partner owned interests, a family trust generally owns 90 percent, with other family members owning the remaining 8 percent in their individual names. This ownership structure is important to obtain the asset protection benefits of the family limited partnership. If all of the partnership interest, both general and limited, were owned by one person or by a husband and wife, then a creditor seeking to attach partnership property would only have to prove that the partnership interests were owned solely by the person (or the person and his or her spouse) in order to attach the assets of the partnership. However, when additional family members own interests in the partnership as well, creditors are generally limited to the charging order and foreclosure remedies discussed above.

One reason for having 90 percent of the family limited partnership owned by a family trust is to take advantage of the estate planning benefits provided by owning your property in a trust. Those benefits usually include the avoidance of probate, privacy, increased control over the disposition of the estate, estate tax-reduction benefits, less likelihood of a successful contest action, etc.

Another good reason for placing this percentage of the limited partnership interest in a living trust is that the beneficiaries of a properly drafted living trust can be changed at any time, and the terms of the trust can be easily amended. Whereas once a limited partnership interest is transferred to a family member, it belongs to them until they give or sell it back. Therefore, the use of a revocable living trust provides additional flexibility to those creating the family limited partnership, without losing any of the asset protection benefits that the family limited partnership was designed to provide.

Drafting Family Limited Partnership Agreements

There are many important things to consider when drafting a family limited partnership. It is important to consider all of the peculiarities inherent in the family relationship of the partners, as well as the specific desires and objectives of those creating the partnership. For example, it is important to provide a mechanism preventing the limited partners from being able to maintain an action for partition of the partnership assets, particularly when those assets include the family home and automobiles.

A partition action is a formal legal proceeding where one or more of the partners of a partnership or owners of an asset go to court to force a sale of the assets that are jointly owned. If they are successful in the action, the court then orders a sale of the property. After the property is sold, the proceeds from the sale are divided among the former joint owners in proportion to their ownership interest in the partnership or property prior to the partition. It is possible to waive the right to maintain an action for partition if the waiver is made prior to or at the same time as the creation of the joint ownership interest.

Table 6 lists important provisions to consider placing into your family limited partnership agreement.

Table 6
Important Drafting Provisions for Family Limited Partnerships

Provision	Description
Anti-Partition Language	The agreement should contain language preventing any partner from maintaining an action for partition as discussed above.
No-Removal of General Partner	The agreement should contain language specifically preventing the limited partners from having the ability to remove the general partner from that position.
Control by General Partner	The agreement should specify the rights and duties of the general partner to control the business of the partnership, buy, sell, and borrow against partnership assets and use them for the general partner's benefit in his or her discretion.
Restrictions on Sale of Limited Partnership Interests	The agreement should contain language limiting the limited partners' ability to sell their interests in the partnership by stating that no interest may be sold for the first five years that the partnership is in effect.
First Right of Refusal	The agreement should contain language giving the general partner a first right of refusal or buy-back option in the event that one of the partners wishes to transfer his or her interest.
Designation of Alternate General Partner	Just as it is wise to designate a successor trustee for a trust or an alternate executor under a will, it is wise to choose an alternate general partner who can serve in the event that the general partner is removed or unable to serve.
Successor General Partner Appointed by Limited Partners	The agreement should provide that if both the initial general partner and the alternate partner are removed or unable to serve, the limited partners may vote to elect a successor general partner.
Limited Partners' Power to Remove Successor General Partner	In case things don't work out with the successor general partner appointed by the limited partners, the agreement should provide that they have the right to remove any general partner appointed by them.

Table 6 cont.

Provision	Description
No Admission of New Partners Without Unanimous Consent of Existing Partners	The agreement should require the unanimous written consent of all existing partners to admit new partners.
Payment of Salary	If the assets that are being transferred into the family limited partnership are necessary for the support of the contributing partner(s), then the agreement should provide for a salary to be paid to the contributing partner unless and until that partner is subject to a judgment, charging order, garnishment order, or similar adversarial circumstance.

Transferring Assets to Your Family Limited Partnership

The most beautifully drafted family limited partnership in the world won't do you a bit of good unless you transfer the assets you want to protect into the partnership. Keep the rules and restrictions discussed in the chapter on the legal uses and limitations in mind as you consider which assets to transfer and when. Remember, it's better to wait until you can legally transfer the assets than to transfer them in violation of the creditor protection laws and risk having the transfers set aside at a later date.

Real Estate

Real estate will usually be transferred to the partnership by executing a grant deed or quitclaim deed transferring the property from the person creating the partnership into the name of the partnership. For purposes of our discussion, it really doesn't matter which type of deed you use, although the quitclaim deed is probably the most common.

A quitclaim deed simply states that you are transferring whatever interest you may have in the property to the transferee with no representations or warranties as to your ownership or right to transfer the property. A grant deed, or warranty deed, transfers property to the transferee but has the added feature of making some sort of representations or warranties to the effect that the transferor has clear title to the property being transferred, as well as the right to make the transfer.

When transferring real estate into your family limited partnership, it is important to consider the effect of the transfer on the property taxes, title insurance, and mortgages, if any, on the property being transferred. Most states provide an exemption from reassessment of the property being transferred where there is only a formal change in the method of holding title to the property and the ownership interests remain the same after the transfer as they were before the transfer. You can usually qualify for an exemption like this by creating the partnership with yourself and whoever else owns the property as the initial general and limited partners in proportion to your ownership interests in the property. Then you can transfer the property into the partnership before transferring the interests to the other people you want to have as limited partners.

Additionally, you should consult with the company that provided the title insurance on your real estate to determine whether the transfer of the property to the limited partnership will void your current title insurance policy. Your title insurance company may agree to extend coverage to include the transfer to your family limited partnership for a small fee.

Finally, you should check your mortgage documents or deed of trust and consult with your lender or real-estate broker to determine whether transferring real property to your family limited partnership will trigger any due-on-sale clauses typically found in modern mortgages. A due-on-sale clause is a clause in your mortgage that provides that the full amount of the mortgage will come due in the event that you transfer your ownership of the property to someone else. If your mortgage or deed of trust has a due-on-sale clause and you do not get your lender's consent to the transfer of the property to your family limited partnership, then you may unwittingly find you have triggered the clause and the entire amount of your mortgage is due. This is of particular importance where you have an interest rate significantly lower than those prevailing in the market at the time of the transfer.

The due-on-sale problem can usually be avoided by contacting your lender and getting permission to transfer the property to your family limited partnership before you make the transfer. Most lenders will be willing to waive the due-on-sale clause for a small fee.

Automobiles

Automobiles must generally be transferred by changing the title on the vehicle from the name of the contributing owner to that of the family limited partnership. This is done through your local division of motor vehicles department. The transferee should be your family limited partnership.

Personal Property

You can transfer all of your personal property to your family limited partnership by executing a bill of sale and assignment similar to the one illustrated in Form 3. This document does not generally need to be recorded or filed with any public office and will serve as evidence of the transfer and the date on which it occurred.

Form 3
Bill of Sale and Assignment

BILL OF SALE AND ASSIGNMENT

This instrument is effective [date] by and between [your name] and [your spouse's name] (hereafter called transferors) and [your name] as the general partner of the [name of your family limited partnership], (hereafter called transferee).

Transferors assign and transfer to transferees all their right, title, and interest in and to all their tangible personal property. The term "tangible personal property" refers, without limitation, to such items as furniture, furnishings, silverware, objects of art, china, clothing, jewelry, sporting equipment, automobiles, books, collections of tangible personal property, and other tangible personal property normally kept at transferor's residence(s). The term "tangible personal property" includes any insurance policies on this tangible personal property and any proceeds of these policies. The term "tangible personal property" excludes cash and other items of intangible personal property, even if represented by tangible documentation of ownership, and also excludes tangible personal property used by either of us in a trade, business, or profession; gold bars; bars of other metals; and any other tangible property of an investment nature (other than art objects and collections of tangible personal property).

TRANSFERORS: TRANSFEREES:

_____   _____

[Transferor's Name]   [Transferee's Name]

_____   _____

[Transferor's Spouse's Name]   [Transferee's Spouse's Name]

Valuing Family Limited Partnership Interests

In addition to its use in asset protection planning, the family limited partnership has been used for years as a valuable estate planning tool. This is because the Internal Revenue Service generally permits discounts in the value of family limited partnership interests that are transferred among family members. These discounts are generally allowed for a lack of marketability of the interests and because the interests are generally minority interests. Interestingly enough, the characteristics that permit tax benefits when transferring family limited partnership interests are the very same characteristics that make family limited partnership interests so unattractive to creditors and such valuable asset protection planning tools.

Professionals Can Assist in Valuing and Completing Transfers

When transferring interests in your family limited partnership to family members, you should consult with a qualified accountant, attorney, or estate planner to determine and comply with the applicable tax-reporting requirements. Additionally, these professionals can provide guidance as to the size of the discount that can be taken when making the transfers based on reported cases of discounts that were permitted to other taxpayers in similar situations with similar properties. As an extra precaution to support the valuation and discount you place on the limited partnership interest you are transferring, you may want to consider retaining the services of a qualified independent appraiser who will provide a value and discount percentage complete with extensive supporting documentation.

One reason that it is important to value the limited partnership interests...is to determine whether there are any estate tax reduction advantages to making the transfers.

Using Family Limited Partnerships to Reduce Income and Estate Taxes

One reason it is important to value the limited partnership interests is to determine whether there are any estate tax reduction advantages to making the transfers. Under the current federal unified estate and gift tax laws, taxpayers are provided with a $600,000 exemption equivalent from federal estate taxes (married taxpayers are provided an exemption equivalent of $1.2 million). This means that no estate and gift taxes will be paid on the first $600,000 of net assets in a decedent's estate. Any assets over that amount will be taxed according to a sliding scale ranging from 37 percent to 60 percent including 5 percent surtax of the net value of the assets.

Knowing this, many people try to reduce their estate prior to their death to an amount just under the $600,000 or $1.2 million exemption equivalent. That way, there is more of their estate for their heirs—and less for the IRS—after their death. By using the discounting technique for valuing family limited partnership interests, it is possible to eliminate or reduce estate taxes that would otherwise be payable on the death of the person creating and contributing property to the limited partnership.

For example, what if you and your spouse had assets totaling $2 million, and you created a family limited partnership for estate planning and asset protection purposes? Let's say you transfer all of your property to the family limited partnership and then transfer substantially all of the limited partnership interests to your children. If you retain a qualified independent appraiser to value the limited partnership interests that are being transferred to your children, it is not at all unlikely that the appraiser would conclude that the lack of control and limited marketability of the partnership interests merited a 40 percent discount from their proportionate value of the $2 million of underlying assets held by the partnership.

If you then transfer the limited partnership interests to the children, you will have effectively eliminated any estate taxes on these assets, as the value of the transfer at $1.2 million ($2 million x 60%) will be within the $1.2 million exemption equivalent. In a 50 percent estate tax bracket, this would result in a net savings of $400,000 ($2 million estate before the transfers - $1.2 million estate after the transfers x 50% tax rate). As you can see, for larger estates, this is a significant estate planning side benefit to asset protection planning using the family limited partnership—one well worth considering.

The Revenue Reconciliation Bill of 1997 contains a proposal to increase the effective exemption from $600,000.00 to $1,000,000.00 with a phase-in beginning in 1998 and completed in 2014.

Questions and Answers about Family Limited Partnerships and the Use of Partnerships in Asset Protection Planning

1. Q: *Do I need any special documents to create a family partnership?*
   A: No, general partnerships can generally be created orally, without signing any special legal papers. However, many of the asset protection benefits of a family partnership can only be obtained by using a carefully drafted, written partnership agreement. In contrast, you need a written family limited partnership agreement to create a family limited partnership.

2. Q: *How much does it cost to create a family limited partnership?*
   A: The prices vary from state to state. Consult your state's Secretary of State to find out the current filing fees for a limited partnership.

3. Q: *How will using a family limited partnership complicate my life?*
   A: When you form the family limited partnership, you will need to file a form with your Secretary of State's office. These forms vary from state to state, and you can determine which forms you need by calling your Secretary of State. Additionally, the family limited partnership will need a federal employer identification number or FEIN, which you can obtain by

completing and mailing an IRS Form SS-4. The family limited partnership is an entity unto itself; therefore, it must file state and federal partnership tax returns. See your accountant or tax advisor for details, or you can get the forms from your local IRS service center.

4. Q: *Can my spouse and I both be general partners of our family limited partnership?*
   A: Yes, you can both be general partners at the same time, or one of you can be the initial general partner and the other can be the alternate general partner.

5. Q: *Will I pay any more income taxes after I form my family limited partnership, or will things stay about the same?*
   A: It depends on who the other partners are. Income will be passed through and taxed to the other partners at their marginal rates, so it is possible that the total taxes would go up if you transfer the property to partners in a higher tax bracket than you are currently in—although after the transfer, your taxes would actually be lower because you would not pay taxes on the interests of the other partners. A much more typical scenario is that the partners to whom the limited partnership interests are transferred are in significantly lower brackets than the transferring partners; therefore both the transferring partners' taxes and the total taxes paid go down.

Quick Quiz—Is a Family Limited Partnership Right for You?

1. Do you have personal assets with a net value of greater than $50,000? __ Yes __ No

2. Do you have one or more children? __ Yes __ No

3. Do you have trustworthy brothers or sisters? __ Yes __ No

4. Is it important to you to be in absolute control of the assets that you put into your family partnership? __ Yes __ No

5. Are you willing to deal with some extra paperwork, record keeping, and tax filings to get the asset protection advantages afforded by a family limited partnership? __ Yes __ No

6. Is the net value of your estate greater than $1.2 million ($600,000 for a single person) at the present time? __ Yes __ No

7. Is it likely that the total net value of your estate will be more than $1.2 million ($600,000 for a single person) in the next five to ten years? __ Yes __ No

8. Do you have or plan to buy insurance with a death benefit that, together to your current net worth, will be more than $1.2 million ($600,000 for a single person)? • __ Yes __ No

9. Are you or your spouse likely to inherit assets from your parents or anyone else that, when combined with your current net worth, would exceed $1.2 million ($600,000 for a single person)? __ Yes __ No

10. Do you own or operate a business as a self-employed person? __ Yes __ No

Scoring: If you answered yes to more than five of the questions above, then you should consider forming a family limited partnership to hold your personal assets.

Chapter Six

Using Domestic Corporations and Limited Liability Companies to Protect Your Business Assets

Corporations have long been a favorite choice of savvy business owners for protecting their personal assets against business related claims and liabilities, and corporations still offer many important benefits not available to owners of sole proprietorships and partnerships. Those benefits are outlined briefly in Table 7.

Table 7
Some Benefits of Corporations over Proprietorships and Partnerships

Benefit	Description
Limited Liability	Unlike partnerships and sole proprietorships where the owners' personal assets are not protected against the claims of business creditors, corporate shareholders' liability for the debts of the corporation is limited to their investment in the corporation's stock
Continuity of Ownership	When a sole proprietor or partner dies, the business generally ceases to exist, but when a shareholder of a corporation dies, the corporation continues—only the ownership of the corporate shares changes
Flexibility in Planning	Corporations generally afford many more planning opportunities for tax reduction through the use of income shifting to persons or entities in lower tax brackets, pension and profit sharing plans, and medical expense reimbursement plans
Separate Identity from Owners	The corporation has its own identity and taxpayer identification number, so if either the corporation or one of its shareholders ever has a credit problem, the other shouldn't be adversely affected

While there are other advantages, they are not as important to asset protection and, therefore, are not discussed in this book.

Limited Liability Companies: The New Kid on the Block

Limited Liability Companies ("LLCs") are a relatively new type of business entity that has gained great popularity and public interest over the past few years. LLCs have some of the best characteristics of corporations combined with some of the best characteristics of partnerships. The result is a wonderful new type of entity that is very attractive for ownership of both business and personal assets.

Table 8
Some Benefits of LLCs

Benefits	Descriptions
Limited Liability	The liability of the members of a LLC is generally limited to their investment in the LLC
Protection From Creditors	The same benefits of a partnership that provide protection for partners from a creditor being able to attach partnership assets to satisfy its claims against an individual partner apply
Less Restrictions Than a Subchapter S Corporation	The Internal Revenue Code places numerous restrictions on subchapter S corporations. For example there can be no more than 75 shareholders, shareholders must be United States citizens and residents, trusts and other corporations may, in most cases not be shareholders, etc. None of these restrictions apply to LLCs
Taxed the Same Way as a Partnership	LLCs avoid the double taxation on corporate profits at the corporate level and dividends at the shareholder level that is present in a regular corporation
No Formal Annual Minutes Required	Unlike corporations, whose limited liability protection can be lost for failure to prepare annual minutes and follow other corporate formalities, the LLC does not require annual minutes.

Differences between Corporations and LLCs

The major differences between corporations and LLCs are highlighted in Table 9. As you can see, the table also points out some applications where you might prefer one of these entities to the other.

Table 9
Differences between Corporations and LLCs

Feature	Corporation	LLC
Limited Liability	Can be destroyed for failure to maintain corporate minutes and formalities.	No formalities required.
Taxation at the Entity Level	Taxed as a separate entity, although pass through partnership-like taxation is available to Subchapter S corporations.	Taxed as a partnership, provided that it has at least two of the characteristics of a corporation. Most state statutes are drafted so that partnership taxation results unless certain changes in the structure of the LLC are made.
Taxation at the Owner Level	Shareholders of regular corporations pay no taxes on the entity's income. They pay taxes on dividends and/or salaries received. This creates the opportunity for shareholders who have income from sources other than the corporation to play the "bracket game" discussed in more detail below. Subchapter S corporations are taxed like partnerships, and shareholders pay taxes on income whether or not it is distributed to them.	The member/owners of a LLC are taxed on the entity's income whether profits are distributed or not. The exception to this rule is if the LLC has more than two of the corporate characteristics, in which case it is taxed as a corporation.
Protection from Creditors of Individual Owners	The corporation is designed more to protect its owners from personal liability for business debts than it is to protect them from liability generated in other areas of their lives. Therefore, a creditor of a shareholder of a corporation will generally be allowed to foreclose on the shareholder's stock in the corporation. After the foreclosure, the creditor becomes an owner of the corporation with all of the rights that any other shareholder would have. This arrangement provides little protection from creditors of individual shareholders of the corporation.	The LLC provides protection from business creditors and personal creditors, because it has the characteristics of a partnership and creditors will find it much more difficult to foreclose on the interest owned by a member of an LLC. Even if the creditor is able to foreclose, options will be very limited because it will own an unmarketable interest in an entity without voting and other rights, unless the remaining members consent to the admission of the creditor as a new member of the LLC.
Formation	Formed by completing articles of incorporation and filing them with the Secretary of State for the state of incorporation. Minutes for shareholder and director meetings must be prepared, as well as by-laws, and stock must be issued to shareholders. Annual minutes of shareholder and director meetings must be prepared thereafter on an annual basis.	Formed by completing articles of organization and filing them with the Secretary of State for the state of organization. An operating agreement detailing the relationships among the member of the LLC must be prepared. There is no continuing obligation to prepare annual minutes.

How Corporations and LLCs Protect Your Assets

...the bracket game...is worth a look for anyone in a tax bracket higher than 15 percent.

Corporations and LLCs protect your assets because of their characteristic of limited liability. LLCs have the additional asset protection advantages of the creditor protection provided by partnerships. Both corporations and LLCs have these characteristic benefits because they are entities created by statute. The state legislatures enacted laws that give these types of entities their asset protection benefits, and all you need to do to take advantage of them is to follow the rules in the applicable states' laws. Creditors who seek to get through the limited liability features of corporations and LLCs have the burden of proving that they should be allowed to pierce the protective limited liability veil for some compelling reason.

The Bracket Game: Using Corporations to Minimize Taxes

One of the advantages discussed above relating to regular corporations is that they are taxed as an entity separate from their shareholder/owners. Since the first $25,000 of corporate income is taxed at only 15 percent, it is possible to save taxes by leaving some money in the corporation when the individual shareholder is in a tax bracket higher than 15 percent. For example, if a corporation earned enough money to pay its sole shareholder a salary that placed her in a 31 percent tax bracket and retained $25,000 within the corporation, then there would be a net tax savings of $4,000 (31% shareholder tax bracket - 15% corporation tax bracket x $25,000 left in corporation) as opposed to paying all of the corporate earnings out to the shareholder. That's the bracket game, and it is worth a look for anyone in a tax bracket higher than 15 percent.

Using Retirement Plans

Another way to use corporations to minimize taxes and obtain asset protection at the same time is to install a publicly administered retirement benefit plan such as a 401(k) plan. These types of plans permit you to contribute a certain amount to the plan each year and take a deduction for the contribution so you don't pay taxes on the income contributed to the plan. That's a nice tax benefit, but did you also know that this type of plan provides an asset protection advantage? Even bankruptcy creditors can't attach this asset for the satisfaction of your debts to them. Private plans offer some asset protection benefits as well. However, you must prove, among other things, that you need the funds for your retirement before you avail yourself of the benefits.

Piercing the Corporate Veil

While corporations provide some protection for your personal assets from the claims of business creditors, there are several ways you can lose that protection. While we have discussed some of these limited liability protection losers in previous sections of this book, Table 10 provides a convenient summary of when a creditor can pierce through the protective corporate veil to seize your personal assets to satisfy the business debts of your corporation.

Table 10
Piercing the Corporate Veil

Reason	Description
Criminal Activity	If you use your corporation to commit a crime, it is unlikely that the fact that you committed the crime under the auspices of a corporation will protect you from personal liability for your actions.
Fraud	Similarly, if you use your corporation to perpetrate a fraud, it is unlikely that the fact that you perpetrated the fraud in the name of the corporation will save your personal assets from exposure to liability for your wrongful actions.
Commingling Funds	When you commingle your personal funds with the corporate funds, then you risk losing the limited liability protection.
Lack of Corporate Formalities	When you fail to keep annual shareholder and director meeting minutes and make necessary annual corporate filings, you risk losing the corporation's limited liability protection.
Alter Ego	When you conduct your business without letting people know that you are doing business as a corporation and otherwise treat the corporation as if you and it were one in the same, then a court may find that the corporation is merely your alter-ego and permit business creditors to look to your personal assets to satisfy their claims.
Personal Guaranties	This is frequently overlooked by corporate shareholders, but be careful that you only sign corporate obligations as an officer of the corporation and not in your own name. Any debts that you incur in your own name, and any corporate obligations that you personally guaranty, will not be avoided by doing business as a corporation and will most likely result in the loss of the limited liability protection otherwise afforded by the corporation.

Tax Consequences of S Corporations, C Corporations, and LLCs

The tax consequences of doing business as a subchapter S corporation, C corporation, or LLC vary and have been discussed in general terms earlier in this chapter. However, it is important to note that each of these forms of doing business carries with it its own particular tax consequences. Therefore, when forming, operating, liquidating, or dissolving these types of entities, it is important to determine the appropriate tax treatment for the type of transaction that the entity is entering into. If you are uncertain of the tax consequences of a particular transaction, then request the applicable publications from the Internal Revenue Service or consult with a tax attorney, CPA, or other tax planning professional.

Using Corporations and LLCs to Reduce State Income Taxes

The tax savings...equal the amount of profits transferred from the heavily taxed state corporation to the tax-free state corporation.

Recent decisions by the courts have created a significant planning opportunity for aggressive taxpayers who live in states with high state income tax brackets (such as California at 11.3 percent) to reduce their state tax obligation by establishing one or more corporations in their own state and one or more corporations in a tax-free or tax-favored state such as Nevada, which has no state corporate income taxes. The strategy is relatively straightforward. You create one corporation in the state in which you live and conduct your business. Then, you create another corporation in a tax-free state. The corporation in the tax-free state then renders services, leases equipment, sells product, loans money, or otherwise provides something of value to the corporation in the heavily taxed state.

The amount charged for the benefit provided from the tax-free state corporation is, ideally, enough to significantly reduce or eliminate the profit of the corporation located in the heavily taxed state. By siphoning off the profits from the heavily taxed state corporation to the tax-free state corporation, you effectively reduce the taxable income of the heavily taxed state corporation to zero. The tax savings then equal the amount of profits transferred from the heavily taxed state corporation to the tax-free state corporation.

For example, assume that a California corporation generates $200,000 in taxable income that would be taxed at the highest marginal California tax bracket of 11.3 percent, prior to a multiple corporation setup. After the setup, a new Nevada corporation provides some benefits for which it can reasonably charge the California corporation $200,000. The net tax savings by using two corporations is $22,600 ($200,000 profit transferred x 11.3% highest California bracket) per year. The money transferred to the tax-free state can then be used for investments or to make additional loans or provide additional goods or services to the California corporation. Of course, any money brought back into California for the personal use of the owners of the corporation or under circumstances other than a legitimate loan, sale, or lease would be in effect "repatriated" to California and subject to the California state income tax.

When establishing a state tax reduction plan such as this it is important to be sure that the amount that your tax-free state corporation is charging to the heavily taxed state corporation is reasonably related to the benefit that is provided. If you cannot justify the fees charged, then you may find yourself liable for the taxes due on the excess profits transferred to the tax-free state in the event of an audit by a state taxing agency. Similarly, it is important to carefully document all of the transactions between the two corporations with loan agreements, promissory notes, security agreements, financing statements, lease agreements, sales agreements, and the like. These documents will provide valuable evidence of the legitimacy of the transactions in the event of an audit.

Table 11
Steps Taken by State Taxing Authorities to Verify Legitimacy of Tax-Free State Corporation

Legitimacy Verification	Ways to Prove Legitimacy
Verify Existence and Good Standing Status of Tax-Free State Corporation with Secretary of State of Tax-Free State.	Incorporate the corporation by filing the Articles of Incorporation and all other required documents with the Secretary of State for the state in which you wish to incorporate it. Then follow through by paying all annual renewal and other fees required to maintain the corporation in good standing.
Verify Address and Contact for Agent for Service of Process in State of Incorporation	Contract with a reputable resident agent service to provide agent services after you incorporate the tax-free state corporation.
Verify Telephone Listing for Tax-Free State Corporation with Directory Assistance	Establish telephone service for the tax-free state corporation with the telephone carrier in a major city in the tax free state.
Verify Yellow Page Listing for Tax-Free State Corporation in Printed Yellow Pages	Maintain a simple, inexpensive yellow pages listing for your business in the yellow pages for the city in the tax-free state listed as the address for your corporation in that state.
Verify Phone Answering for Tax-Free State Corporation	Secure a telephone answering service to answer the phones for your tax-free state corporation.
Verify Business License for Tax-Free State Corporation	Secure a business license for your new corporation in the city listed as its address on the corporate filings.
Verify Bank Account Maintained by Tax-Free State Corporation	Open a bank account in the name of your new tax-free state corporation.
Visit Office of Tax-Free State Corporation to Verify Physical Facilities	Rent a headquarters type office suite for your tax-free state corporation.

Finally, when implementing a state tax reduction strategy such as this, keep in mind that it is important for the tax-free state corporation to be more than just a shell. In the event of an audit, the state taxing agency's auditors will most likely take the steps listed in Table 11 to verify the existence and legitimacy of your tax-free state corporation. Therefore, you should take the proactive protective step provided in the second column to anticipate and address the attempt to show that your tax-free state corporation is just a way to avoid paying state taxes.

While the protective steps listed above may seem like a lot, many companies provide all of the services described as part of a corporate identity package for as little as $2,000 per year. A thorough investigation of the offerings in the tax-free state of your choice should reveal many such providers, and you may even be able to negotiate more favorable pricing if you are willing to sign a long term agreement. Remember to sign it in the name of one of your corporations and not personally!

Where to Incorporate to Maximize Tax and Asset Protection Benefits

Many people believe that the best place to incorporate is Delaware. That's a pretty good choice, but if just you, or you and a few other people own an incorporated business, you don't need to be a Delaware corporation. Delaware corporations are popular with large companies due to a well-established body of case law regarding corporate issues and favorable Delaware laws that protect existing management of corporations from attacks of unhappy shareholders. Unless you are planning on defending a shareholder derivative lawsuit, a hostile takeover, tender offer, or a heated proxy fight for corporate control, chances are you don't need a Delaware corporation for your business.

A better choice for asset protection is probably a state like Nevada, with no corporate income taxes, favorable laws for corporate owners, and a Secretary of State who has refused to cooperate with the Internal Revenue Service in providing certain records regarding corporations. Nevada law also permits the issuance of bearer shares. Bearer shares are stock certificates representing an ownership interest in a corporation that state that whoever is holding the share (the bearer) is the owner. Bearer shares provide additional asset protection planning opportunities, discussed in greater detail in the chapter on trusts.

Using Corporations and LLCs to Reduce Estate Taxes

The discussion in Chapter Five on using partnerships to reduce estate taxes applies equally to corporations and LLCs. By taking advantage of minority interest and lack of marketability discounts, the shareholders of corporations and members of LLCs can achieve significant estate tax reduction and estate planning benefits.

Professional Corporations and Limited Liability Partnerships

Certain professionals who want to incorporate are required by the laws of their states to incorporate as a special kind of corporation called a professional corporation. Usually, professionals such as accountants, doctors, lawyers, and other licensed professionals fall into this category. Professional corporations generally provide only very limited asset protection benefits. They are usually used in situations where groups of professionals join together to provide services, and one or more members of the group wants protection from any professional negligence by other members of the group. By forming a professional corporation, each member can limit his or her liability for negligence of the other members of the group. You may have seen this on professional stationery abbreviated as P.C. or A.P.C., a partnership of professional corporations.

State laws usually prohibit the use of a professional corporation to avoid personal liability for professional negligence for the acts of the person providing the professional services. Therefore, the professional corporation is an ineffective tool for providing personal asset protection. If you are a member of a group that may only operate in the corporate form as a professional corporation, it is extremely important to take the necessary steps to protect your personal assets from the claims of creditors, since any professional corporation you form will not protect you from claims based on your professional negligence.

Limited Liability Partnerships or LLPs are another liability limiting type of entity which have been authorized recently by many states. These entities offer many advantages not offered by Professional Corporations, chief among them being the ability to escape personal liability for personal negligence. Because this is a very new form of entity, we will have to wait to see how court cases involving LLP partners are decided and how effectively this entity form is in protecting assets. Check with your Secretary of State to see if this business form is available to you in your state and what the costs and limitations are.

Questions and Answers about Corporations and LLCs

1. Q: *Do I need to use a corporation or LLC in my asset protection plan if I don't own my own business?*
   A: No, you can probably get all of the asset protection planning benefits that you need by using a family partnership or family limited partnership.

2. Q: *Based on your experience, which form of entity do you most highly recommend, corporations or LLCs?*
   A: It really depends on the state legislation for the state in which you want to form one of these entities. Some states, like California, place many

restrictions and extra charges on LLCs. For example, California doesn't permit LLCs for professionals and charges a tax on gross sales that can result in as much as $4,500 in extra fees for doing business as a LLC. Since a family partnership or family limited partnership can be used to protect your personal assets without these restrictions and extra charges, and the extra benefits of an LLC over a corporation used with partnerships are not that great, the LLC is not a particularly compelling choice of entity in California—at least not for asset protection planning.

3. Q: *How hard is it for someone to "pierce the corporate veil" of a corporation to get to my personal assets?*
   A: Not very hard. There seems to be a trend to permit plaintiffs to pierce the corporate veil to get to shareholders' personal assets whenever the courts determine that it seems like the "fair" thing to do. This represents an erosion of the formerly formidable corporate limited liability fortress, and it means that you better do more than operate your business as a corporation if you want to protect your personal assets from the claims of business creditors.

   If you have a small, closely held corporation, it's very likely that you will be the one who actually did whatever it is that caused a plaintiff to sue. The lawyer for the plaintiff will almost always name you as a defendant in addition to the corporation, and if he or she can convince the judge and/or jury that your personal actions caused the damage being sued for, then there's a good chance that both you and your corporation will be held liable. If you are held liable, your personal assets will be available to satisfy any judgment awarded to the plaintiff.

4. Q: *Are LLCs available in all states?*
   A: Not as of the printing of this book, but state legislatures in all states are considering LLC legislation, so check with your Secretary of State if you're not sure.

5. Q: *How do I go about finding someone to provide me with an office space, phone answering, and mail forwarding service in the city in the tax-free state where my corporation's registered agent is located?*
   A: If you're having trouble with this, try ordering a newspaper from the city where you're trying to find this service and checking the classifieds under office space, commercial space, office suites, or mini-suites. You will probably find many listings for national office suite companies like HQ, as well as local companies eager to provide this service. When you call these services to check rates, tell them that all you need is phone answering, a listing on the building directory, a directory assistance listing, a yellow pages listing, mail forwarding, and an occasional office for one or two hours per month. They should then be able to give you a

quote ranging from \$100–\$300 per month for this service, but you can probably negotiate a better rate if you're willing to sign a long-term (1 year or more) contract or to prepay the entire lease.

Quick Quiz—Should You Use a Corporation or LLC in Your Plan?

1. Do you own all or part of a business? ___ Yes ___ No

2. Does your business have employees? ___ Yes ___ No

3. Does your business provide professional services? ___ Yes ___ No

4. Do you play a significant role in performing the services provided by your business? ___ Yes ___ No

5. Do you face the risk of being sued for professional negligence? ___ Yes ___ No

6. Does your business advertise? ___ Yes ___ No

7. Does your business deal in any intellectual property, such as copyrights, trademarks, or patents, whether creating, marketing, selling, buying, or wholesaling products or services that involve such intellectual property? ___ Yes ___ No

8. Does your business own or lease real property, the land or buildings of which could now be, or in the past have been, contaminated or otherwise contain environmentally unsafe or toxic materials? ___ Yes ___ No

9. Does your business ever experience employee injuries from the operation of any equipment, whether typewriters and computers (carpal tunnel syndrome and radiation exposure) or heavy equipment (loss of sight, cuts, dismemberment)? ___ Yes ___ No

10. Is insurance not available or not available in adequate and affordable amounts to cover all of the risks faced by your business? ___ Yes ___ No

Scoring: If you answered yes to five or more of the questions in the quick quiz above, then you should consider placing your business assets into a corporation or LLC to provide asset protection to your personal assets.

Chapter Seven

Using Foreign Corporations to Protect Personal and/or Business Assets

Now that we've discussed partnerships, domestic corporations, and LLCs, we're ready to explore the exotic world of foreign corporations and how they can be used to enhance the protection afforded by your asset protection plan. A foreign corporation is technically defined as any corporation formed under the laws of a state or country other than the state that you live in. However, for purposes of this chapter, when we refer to a foreign corporation we are talking about one that is formed outside the United States.

How Foreign Corporations Can Bullet Proof Your Assets

Over the past few years, the foreign corporation has enjoyed increasing popularity as an asset protection tool. The main reason for this is that foreign corporations are outside the jurisdiction of the United States courts, and many foreign countries do not recognize judgments obtained against their corporations in a United States court. This means that creditors may find it extremely difficult to collect and enforce judgments they obtain against a foreign corporation that has no connections to the United States beyond ownership by United States shareholders.

Advantages and Disadvantages of Using a Foreign Corporation

The advantages and disadvantages of using a foreign corporation in your asset protection plan are summarized in Table 12.

Table 12
Advantages and Disadvantages of Using Foreign Corporations in Your Plan

Advantages	Disadvantages
Minimal Public Disclosure of Corporate Information - Many foreign countries have enacted secrecy laws and do not provide the names of officers, directors, or shareholders of foreign corporations as part of any publicly available records.	**Require Trust** - Using a foreign corporation requires you to trust someone located in the foreign country to, at a minimum, serve as your registered agent. Additionally, depending on your asset protection plan, you may also need to trust a foreign agent to act as an officer, director, shareholder, or even bank account signatory.
No or Low Taxes - Most of the more popular foreign countries for asset protection planning have no or very low tax rates for foreign corporations that do not conduct the bulk of their business within the foreign country.	**Long Distance Relationships** - When you deal with people in a foreign country, you must deal with the inevitable delays brought about by doing business long distance, including time zone differences, poor telecommunications infrastructures, and longer postal turn around times.
Flexibility of Ownership - To provide flexibility to the owners of stock in corporations incorporated in their countries, the most appealing asset protection jurisdictions permit "bearer shares," which are owned by whoever holds the shares at any given time.	**Expensive to Establish** - Foreign corporations can be significantly more costly to establish than domestic corporations.
Access to World-Class Banking Services - As major offshore financial centers, most of the asset protection favored countries are home to hundreds of banks based out of every major country in the world, including Switzerland, England, France, Hong Kong, and the United States, to name a few.	**Expensive to Maintain** - Foreign corporations may also be more expensive to maintain than their U.S. counterparts.
Flexibility of Directors - To provide even greater flexibility in the management and direction of businesses incorporated in their countries, many of the preferred asset protection countries permit corporations, as opposed to individuals, to act as the directors of their corporations, providing added protection and secrecy to the shareholders of the director corporations. Additionally, these corporations may be nominees who are named as directors solely for the convenience of the true directors, whose instructions the nominees must follow.	**Extensive U.S. Reporting Obligations** - Anyone who establishes, operates, controls, or contributes property to a foreign corporation may be faced with significant tax and other reporting obligations. See the chart in Chapter 2 for more details. Failure to comply can result in civil and criminal penalties.

Table 12 cont.

Advantages	Disadvantages
Flexibility of Officers - The same flexibility provided by permitting corporate and nominee directors is provided by those countries whose laws also permit corporate and nominee officers for businesses incorporated in their countries.	**Annual Reports** - Some foreign countries attempt to stimulate their local economies by requiring you to hire a local accountant to prepare an annual report that must be filed with the foreign country's government.
Minimal or No Cooperation with U.S. Government - Many of the more favored asset protection planning countries either have no treaties requiring them to cooperate with the U.S. government, or they have treaties that are limited to providing information to only certain U.S. government entities for certain limited purposes.	**Other Tax Concerns** - Using foreign corporations brings into play many U.S. tax laws designed to prevent tax abuses by those attempting to escape liability for U.S. taxes. These laws are discussed in greater detail later in this chapter.
Minimal or No Recognition of U.S. Judgments - Because they enjoy the asset protection business generated by their favorable laws, most of the preferred asset protection planning countries do not recognize judgments obtained in U.S. courts and do not cooperate with U.S. creditors seeking to enforce claims against foreign corporate debtors.	**Unfamiliar Local Laws** - The laws of most of the foreign countries whose corporations are used for asset protection planning are unfamiliar to U.S. citizens, who may unwittingly run afoul of them.
Other Favorable Laws - Other favorable foreign laws may establish shorter statutes of limitations for challenging transactions to foreign based corporations, require creditors to sue in the country in which the corporation was incorporated, establish extremely high burdens of proof for creditors, and require creditors to post a bond before being allowed to sue.	**Stigma** - When conducting business through a foreign corporation, you may experience some reluctance from U.S. businesses whom you ask to contract with and/or make payments to your foreign corporation. Even if they can't give you a good reason for their reluctance, they may simply say that it just doesn't feel or "smell" right to do business with a foreign corporation.

Most people who have liquid assets of less than $100,000 should avoid using foreign corporations in their asset protection plan, because the costs and headaches outweigh the benefits foreign corporations provide. However, if you have $100,000 or more in cash, certificates of deposit, stocks, bonds, mutual funds, and/or similar liquid assets, then you should explore further the possibility of using a foreign corporation in your asset protection planning. You may find that the secrecy and protection offered by these corporations outweighs any disadvantages.

How Foreign Corporations Fit into Your Asset Protection Plan

If you do decide to use a foreign corporation as part of your asset protection plan, remember that it is only one part of your plan. You should integrate it within your plan to work in conjunction with the other strategies and tools discussed in this book. For example, rather than creating a foreign corporation to own all of your assets outright, consider layering the ownership of the assets by forming a family limited partnership to own your personal assets and a regular domestic corporation to own your business assets. The interests of the family limited partnership could then be owned by your foreign corporation, as could the stock of your domestic corporation. Using this layering technique you can obtain additional privacy and create more hoops for your creditors to jump through to get to your assets.

Reducing U.S. Income Taxes on Foreign Income

If you have any income from countries other than the United States, you may be able to use a foreign corporation to reduce your U.S. income taxes on that foreign income. This is accomplished by structuring the ownership and operation of the foreign corporation so that the United States has no federal income tax jurisdiction over the foreign corporation's income. It is not enough to simply form a foreign corporation owned by you or your nominees and claim that no U.S. income taxes are due on income generated by that foreign corporation. There are numerous provisions in the U.S. Internal Revenue Code to "catch" this income and make it taxable to you.

Keep in mind that these laws are in a constant state of change, so check with an attorney or accountant well-versed in international tax law before using your foreign corporation to achieve any tax benefits.

Reducing U.S. Income Taxes on Income Generated in the United States

While it is more difficult to use your foreign corporation to reduce U.S. income taxes on income generated in the United States, it is possible under certain circumstances. If you have any form of intellectual property, you may be able to transfer that property to a foreign corporation and pay the foreign corporation royalties for the use of that property from your U.S. corporation. Intellectual property can include patents, copyrights, trademarks, service marks, trade secrets, and trade dress. These types of intellectual property cover a broad range of things including plans, specifications, designs, drawings, books, tapes, videos, franchises, business systems, formulas, package design, advertising copy, inventions, and other items.

The secret to making a plan to reduce taxes on U.S. generated income work is to carefully structure the plan to avoid the traps the government designed to catch the unwary. Stay abreast of recent developments in the numerous laws that apply to these types of plans, and clearly establish and document the values of assets transferred, the transfers themselves, and the uses of the property transferred by your domestic corporation.

Again, keep in mind that these laws are in a constant state of change, so check with an attorney or accountant well versed in international tax law before using your foreign corporation to achieve any tax benefits.

Tax Laws to Be Aware of

There are numerous federal tax laws to be aware of and watch for when using foreign corporations as a component of your asset protection plan. A brief summary of some of the most important ones is provided in Table 13. Keep in mind that these

Table 13
Tax Laws to Be Aware of

Tax Law	Description
Controlled Foreign Corporation Rules ("CFC")	Internal Revenue Code §957 defines a CFC as a foreign corporation where more than 50 percent of the voting power or value is owned by U.S. shareholders on any day of the taxable year of that foreign corporation. CFC's may be subject to U.S. taxes.
Foreign Personal Holding Company Rules ("FPHC")	Section 552(a) of the Internal Revenue Code defines a FPHC, with some exceptions, as a foreign corporation with at least 60 percent of its gross income for the taxable year consisting of foreign personal company income, provided that at any time during the taxable year more than 50 percent of the corporation's value or voting power is owned, directly or indirectly, by not more than five (5) individuals who are citizens or residents of the United States. The FPHC rules subject U.S. shareholders to tax on all undistributed taxable income of the foreign corporation.
Not-Effectively Connected Withholding Rules	Internal Revenue Code §881(a) imposes a 30 percent withholding tax on certain kinds of income not effectively connected with a U.S. trade or business. This tax is imposed on gross amounts received by a foreign corporation without allowance for any deductions. Reg. §1.881-2(a)(2) and Reg. §1.881-2(a)(3).
Passive Foreign Investment Company Rules	Internal Revenue Code §§1291-1297 subject the income from foreign corporations with 75 percent or more of gross income comprising of passive income or with 50 percent or more passive-income producing assets to current taxation. As always, exceptions may apply.
Excise Tax on Transfers of Appreciated Assets To Foreign Entity	Subject to several exceptions, Internal Revenue Code §1491 imposes a 35 percent excise tax on any unrealized gain on the transfer of appreciated property to certain foreign entities. Care should be taken to assure that this tax does not apply to transfers to your foreign corporation.

laws are in a constant state of change, so check with an attorney or accountant well-versed in international tax law before using your foreign corporation to achieve any tax benefits.

Using Nominee Officers, Directors, and Shareholders to Gain Privacy and Reduce Your Exposure to Liability

As was mentioned in the table on the advantages and disadvantages of using foreign corporations, the use of nominee officers and directors is permitted by most of the countries that have favorable asset protection laws. Additionally, most of these countries permit corporations to act as officers and directors of corporations incorporated in their jurisdictions. Nominee officers and directors provide you with additional protection and privacy by placing one more obstacle between you and creditors who attempt to attack your asset protection plan.

For example, if you use nominee officers and directors and you don't serve as either an officer or director of your foreign corporation, then you can truthfully testify under oath in a deposition or debtor's examination that you occupy no officer or director positions in the corporation. If you also have the corporation issue bearer shares and have those shares held by a nominee shareholder, you will also be able to testify that you do not own any stock in the corporation. Faced with these answers and no way to verify your answers because of the secrecy laws of the country in which you incorporated the corporation, your creditor is left without any evidence to support any further actions against your foreign corporation. At that point, you are in a position to negotiate a favorable settlement with the creditor to settle its claim and resolve the dispute.

Questions and Answers about Foreign Corporations

1. Q: *I have about $500,000 in net worth, but it's all tied up in U.S. real estate. Should I use a foreign corporation to hold the property?*
    A: Probably not. If the assets that you want to protect are not portable, that is, not capable of being moved outside of this country, then a U.S. court will probably be able to get jurisdiction over the assets, and a foreign corporation won't be as helpful as a family limited partnership or other asset protection strategies.

2. Q: *How much does it cost to set up a foreign corporation?*
    A: It depends on where you incorporate and who you use to do the incorporating. U.S. based attorneys and consultants may charge $10,000 or more, while services located in the foreign countries themselves may charge less than $700. Clearly, it's a good idea to shop around.

3. Q: *If I periodically perform services outside the United States, can I separate my income from those services and avoid paying U.S. taxes on them?*

   A: Probably not. It is extremely difficult for U.S. resident citizens to separate their foreign personal services income from other income to reduce U.S. taxes. However, if foreign taxes are paid on or withheld from that income, you may be entitled to credit for foreign taxes paid.

4. Q: *Can I transfer my copyrights and trademarks to a new foreign corporation for little or no money and then charge myself a high license fee to reduce my taxable income in the United States?*

   A: Probably not. If you have existing copyrights and trademarks that have value, you will have difficulty justifying the transfer for little or no money and the immediate license of those same properties to your U.S. corporation for a high price. It is much better to physically create the intellectual property outside the United States under an agreement where the ownership of the property is immediately vested in the foreign corporation. That way, no transfer is required, and you won't have to justify a substantial discrepancy between the transfer price and the licensing price. Additionally, this strategy avoids many other pitfalls beyond the scope of this discussion.

5. Q: *Are there any tax laws that apply to the pricing of products between my U.S. corporation and my foreign corporation?*

   A: Yes. Internal Revenue Code §482 and the U.S. Income Tax Regulations relating to it apply to transfers between related corporations and provide detailed formulas for computing transfer prices.

6. Q: *If my property is located in a foreign country, is there any chance of my U.S. creditors getting to it?*

   A: Yes. No plan is completely impenetrable, but if you incorporate in a country that has no treaties with the United States and does not recognize U.S. judgments, then it will be very difficult for your creditors to get to your property. For example, if your creditor sues you in Nevis, proves its case beyond a reasonable doubt, posts a bond prior to suing, sues within the short statute of limitations periods provided by Nevis law, and wins, it will probably succeed in attaching assets held by your Nevis corporation, provided that they are located in Nevis. However, it is possible that the liquid assets held by the Nevis corporation would be held in another country which recognized neither United States nor Nevis court judgments. Your creditor would then be required to go to that country and start all over again, and by that time, the assets may have been relocated to yet another country. The creditor is left with mounting attorneys' fees and no tangible results for its efforts. Eventually, the creditor should be willing to accept a favorable settlement of its claim or give up the chase.

7. Q: *Could I be put in jail for failing to cooperate with a U.S. court that ordered me to pay a creditor?*

   A: Yes, in some circumstances you may be ordered by a U.S. court to take certain actions to make your assets available to your creditors. If you ignore or otherwise fail to comply with the court order, you may be held in contempt of court. Contempt of court can subject you to imprisonment until you comply with the court order. If you do not have the power to make your assets available to creditors, a contempt order is much less likely than if you do. For example, if you have the sole signature authority over a foreign bank account controlled by your foreign corporation and a U.S. court orders you, a U.S. citizen and resident, to write a check to your creditor, then you might be jailed for failing to comply with that order. However, if you did not have that signature authority, then a contempt order would be much less likely and, if issued, would be subject to being overturned on appeal.

8. Q: *How do I find out which countries have tax treaties with the United States and which ones don't?*

   A: You can call or write to the U.S. Secretary of State, the Internal Revenue Service, or the Treasury Department. Commerce Clearing House also publishes a guide to U.S. tax treaties.

9. Q: *How do I find out more about the laws of the foreign countries in which I might consider incorporating?*

   A: You can call or write the governments of those countries or their embassies located in the United States (if any).

10. Q: *I'm concerned about putting my money into a bank account in a foreign country. Do all countries have insured bank accounts like we do in the United States?*

    A: No. You should check with the banks of any foreign countries in which you are considering opening bank accounts and placing funds to determine whether and in what amounts insurance is available.

Quick Quiz—Should You Use a Foreign Corporation in Your Plan

1. Do you have liquid assets of more than $100,000? __ Yes __ No

2. Are you prepared to spend $10,000 or more to set up and implement a foreign component to your asset protection plan? __ Yes __ No

3. Are you prepared to spend $1,500 - $5,000 per year to maintain your foreign corporations and nominees, if any? __ Yes __ No

4. Are you willing to file all of the necessary documents with the Internal Revenue Service when establishing the foreign component to your asset protection plan? __ Yes __ No

5. Are you willing to accept the risk of having your assets in stable but uninsured banks? __ Yes __ No

6. Can you afford to wait 10–15 days to access your foreign representatives for signatures on documents and the like? __ Yes __ No

7. Can you afford to wait for U.S. checks or wires to be processed through to your foreign accounts (10–15 days)? __ Yes __ No

8. Are you willing to periodically travel to the country where you will incorporate your foreign corporation? __ Yes __ No

9. Are you willing to prepare the extra tax returns and filings associated with having a foreign corporation? __ Yes __ No

10. Are you comfortable with an aggressive tax and asset protection strategy? __ Yes __ No

Scoring: Unless you answered yes to all ten of the questions above, a foreign corporation is probably not right for you. People who use foreign corporations for asset protection planning and tax reduction must be willing to take and defend an aggressive tax position with the Internal Revenue Service. They must be willing to complete all reporting and compliance filings when the corporation is created and as it continues to operate. Delays of ten to fifteen days are common when dealing with overseas banks and representatives. If you aren't comfortable with or can't afford to have such delays, you should avoid the use of a foreign corporation.

However, for those who can deal with the extra complications of having a foreign corporation, the tax reduction and asset protection benefits can be substantial. While no plan is ever completely risk free, plans that use foreign corporations do offer the greatest protection for your assets.

Chapter Eight

Using Trusts in Asset Protection Planning

Just as the use of partnerships and corporations in your asset protection plan can provide additional protection and benefits, so can the use of domestic and foreign trusts. Trusts have been around in one form or another for hundreds of years and can be used for everything from simple probate avoidance to complex estate planning, asset protection, and tax reduction strategies.

What Trusts Are and How They Work

A trust is nothing more than a contract between two or more people for the ownership, control, and management of property. The person who creates the trust is called the grantor, settlor, or trustor. The person who receives the benefits of the trust is called the beneficiary, and the person who runs the show and operates the trust is called the trustee. There can be one or more grantors, beneficiaries, and/or trustees.

The trust agreement—also sometimes called the declaration of trust—says that the grantor has contributed property to the trust for the benefit of the beneficiary and that the grantor would like the trustee to manage the property in accordance with the instructions the grantor provided in the trust agreement. After accepting the position as trustee, the trustee must run the trust in accordance with the grantor's instructions or face being removed by either the grantor or the beneficiary. If the trustee mismanages the trust or uses trust property for the trustee's benefit without permission from the grantor and/or beneficiary, then the grantor or beneficiary can sue the trustee for breach of trust, remove the trustee, and seek damages.

Trusts can be either revocable or irrevocable. Revocable trusts can be amended or modified by the grantor at any time prior to the grantor's death. That means that the grantor can change the trustee, change the beneficiary, add or remove trust provisions, or completely undo the trust and recover any property contributed to it. Irrevocable trusts cannot be amended or modified after they are created, and even the grantor can't change trustees, beneficiaries, or trust provisions unless the trust agreement permits it.

How the Use of Trusts Can Provide Additional Asset Protection Benefits

Using a trust as part of your asset protection plan can provide additional protection by placing another layer between you and your creditors and by transferring your power to control your assets to a trustee. Because a trust is a separate entity from you, it can own property in its own name. If you transfer the ownership of property from your name into the name of the trust, then it is no longer available to your creditors to satisfy your debts. If you use trusts as a component of your asset protection plan and integrate them with the other strategies and tools discussed in this book, they can be a valuable part of your overall asset protection plan.

For example, let's assume that you decide to form a family limited partnership to own your personal assets and a domestic corporation to own your business assets. Also assume that your foreign corporation owns all the stock in your domestic corporation. If you then form an irrevocable asset protection trust to own the limited partnership interest in your family limited partnership and the stock of your foreign corporation, you have placed many obstacles in the path of any creditor who comes looking for your assets to satisfy claims against you. Using the trust as part of an integrated asset protection strategy this way helps provide additional protection for your assets.

Why Living Trusts Provide No Asset Protection

To get the asset protection benefits of using a trust you have to use an irrevocable trust. If you use a trust that you have the power to revoke, then your creditors are, by law, permitted to reach into the trust and use its assets to satisfy their claims against you. That's why a regular living trust—the kind you see advertised as a way to avoid probate upon your death—is virtually worthless as an asset protection tool. These trusts are revocable during your lifetime. Therefore, creditors can penetrate the trust and recover its assets to satisfy your debts. While you can insert "spendthrift" language into the trust to protect your beneficiaries from the claims of their creditors unless and until those beneficiaries are entitled to a distribution from the trust, you are generally not permitted to use this kind of provision to protect yourself. Additionally, recent cases have permitted the IRS to access trust assets of a beneficiary despite spendthrift provisions contained in the trust.

Domestic v. Foreign Trusts—Which One Is Right for You?

The differences between domestic trusts and foreign trusts are very similar to those between domestic and foreign corporations. Table 14 explains the advantages and disadvantages of using foreign trusts in your asset protection planning.

Table 14
Advantages and Disadvantages of Foreign Trusts

Advantages	Disadvantages
Minimal Public Disclosure of Trust Information - Many foreign countries have enacted secrecy laws and do not provide the names of grantors, beneficiaries, or trustees of foreign trusts as part of any publicly available records.	**Require Trust** - Depending on your asset protection plan, you may need to trust a foreign agent to act as an nominee trustee, trustee, consultant, manager, or bank signatory for your foreign trust.
No or Low Taxes - Most of the more popular foreign countries for asset protection planning have no or very low tax rates for foreign trusts that do not conduct the bulk of their business within the foreign country.	**Long Distance Relationships** - When you deal with people in a foreign country you must deal with the inevitable delays brought about by doing business long distance, including time zone differences, poor telecommunications infrastructures, and longer postal turn around times.
Access to World Class Banking Services - As major offshore financial centers, most of the asset protection favored countries are home to hundreds of banks based out of every major country in the world, including Switzerland, England, France, Hong Kong, and the United States, to name a few.	**Expensive to Establish** - Foreign trusts can be significantly more costly to establish than domestic trusts.
Minimal or No Cooperation with United States Government - Many of the more favored asset protection planning countries either have no treaties requiring them to cooperate with the U.S. government, or they have treaties which are limited to providing information to only certain U.S. government entities for certain limited purposes.	**Expensive to Maintain** - Foreign trusts may also be more expensive than their U.S. counterparts to maintain.
Minimal or No Recognition of U.S. Judgments - Because they enjoy the asset protection business generated by their favorable laws, most of the preferred asset protection planning countries do not recognize judgments obtained in U.S. courts and do not cooperate with U.S. creditors seeking to enforce claims against foreign debtors.	**Extensive U.S. Reporting Obligations** - Anyone who establishes, operates, controls, or contributes property to a foreign trust may be faced with significant tax and other reporting obligations. See the chart in Chapter 2 for more details. Failure to comply can result in civil and criminal penalties.

Table 14 cont.

Advantages	Disadvantages
Short Statutes of Limitations - Foreign laws may establish short statutes of limitations for challenging transfers to foreign based trusts.	**Other Tax Concerns** - Using foreign trusts brings into play many U.S. tax laws designed to prevent tax abuses by those attempting to escape liability for U.S. taxes.
Creditors Must Sue in Country where Trust Was Formed - Most of the countries preferred for asset protection trust formation require creditors to sue the trust in that country, creating additional headaches and expenses for creditors.	**Unfamiliar Local Laws** - The laws of most of the foreign countries whose trusts are used for asset protection planning are unfamiliar to U.S. citizens, who may unwittingly run afoul of them.
High Standard for Burden of Proof - Most countries preferred for asset protection trusts establish extremely high standards for the burden of proof for creditors to win their cases. Some require creditors to prove their case beyond a reasonable doubt—the same high standard used for criminal trials in the United States.	**Stigma** - When conducting business through a foreign trust, you may experience some reluctance from U.S. businesses whom you ask to contract with and/or make payments to your foreign trust. Even if they can't give you a good reason for their reluctance, they may simply say that it just doesn't feel or "smell" right to do business with a foreign trust.
Requirement to Post Bond Prior to Suit - Many countries require creditors to post a bond before being allowed to sue at all.	

Using Fictitious Name Trusts

Even if you decide not to use a foreign trust and an irrevocable trust seems too permanent for you, you should consider using a fictitious name trust. Just as forming a regular corporation with a name different from yours provides some protection, using a fictitious name trust offers you additional asset protection, unless someone knows that it's your trust, it won't put them on notice that you are the grantor, trustee, or beneficiary of the trust. If you choose to use this type of trust, you will need to file a fictitious business name filing with the appropriate government office in the city or county in which the trust will operate. Since fictitious name filings are generally available to the public, you may want to have someone with a different name than yours make the initial filing and then assign it to you without recording the assignment.

Using Sprinkling Trusts

If you do want to use an irrevocable trust but are afraid to because you think you might change your mind about which beneficiaries get what, you may be a candidate for a sprinkling trust. A sprinkling trust is an irrevocable trust that gives the trustee the power to distribute the income and assets of the trust to one or more beneficiaries listed in whatever proportion the trustee desires, whether it's one dollar or one million dollars. If you use a friendly trustee who is willing to follow your wishes, you can transfer your property into a sprinkling trust, provide a list of beneficiaries, and keep the trustee updated on what your desires are. The trustee cannot be obligated to follow your instructions, but you could possibly retain the power to remove the trustee and appoint a substitute or give that removal power to someone else. Additionally, it is possible to reserve the power to add beneficiaries to the trust.

Using Nominee Trustees to Reduce Exposure to Liability

As was mentioned in the table on the advantages and disadvantages of using foreign trusts, the use of nominee trustees is permitted by most of the countries that have favorable asset protection laws. Additionally, most of these countries permit corporations to act as trustees of trusts formed in their jurisdictions. Nominee trustees provide you with additional protection and privacy by placing one more obstacle between you and creditors who attempt to attack your asset protection plan.

For example, if you use nominee trustees and don't serve as a cotrustee of your foreign trust, then you can truthfully testify under oath in a deposition or debtor's examination that you occupy no trustee positions in the trust. Faced with this answer and no way to verify your answer because of the secrecy laws of the country in which you formed the trust, your creditor is left without evidence to support any further actions against your foreign trust. At that point, you are in a position to negotiate a favorable settlement with the creditor to settle its claim and resolve the dispute.

Questions and Answers about Using Trusts in Asset Protection Planning

1. Q: *We have a family trust we set up to avoid probate, reduce estate taxes, and protect our assets. Doesn't it provide us with all the asset protection we need?*
   A: Probably not. Any trust that is revocable is available to your creditors. Since most typical living trusts created for probate avoidance and estate planning purposes are revocable, they offer no real asset protection.

2. Q: *What happens if I set up an irrevocable trust and then want to change something?*
   A: You can't make any changes to an irrevocable trust after it's set up, unless you, the trustee(s), and all beneficiaries agree to the changes you want to make. Don't set up an irrevocable trust unless you are certain you can accept its terms.

3. Q: *What happens if the trustee of my irrevocable trust starts doing things that I don't like? Do I have to accept it?*

   A: Yes, unless you reserve the right to change the trustee or the trustee dies, resigns, or commits a breach of trust, you will probably be stuck with him or her for a long time. Don't set up a trust like this without having complete faith in the trustee and reserving the right for yourself or someone else to change the trustee.

4. Q: *What if my family situation changes so that five years after I set up the irrevocable trust, I don't want to leave the same assets to the beneficiaries I originally designated in the trust? Is there any way to anticipate and prepare for this possibility?*

   A: Yes. If you insert sprinkling powers in your trust and reserve the power to add beneficiaries, you can accomplish this goal. Sprinkling trusts contain a list of potential beneficiaries among whom the trustee is given the power to distribute assets in the trustee's sole discretion. If you have a friendly trustee, you can suggest to the trustee how the sprinkling power should be used, and he or she should be willing to honor your wishes. However, keep in mind that the trustee is not, and cannot be, required to follow your wishes.

5. Q: *Are there any extra taxes for doing business as a trust?*

   A: No, trusts are generally taxed as pass-through entities where the beneficiaries pay income taxes based on their proportionate share of trust income.

6. Q: *Are there any additional tax filings required of trusts, which I don't have to file as an individual?*

   A: Yes. Your trust will probably have to file an IRS Form 1041.

7. Q: *If I decide to use an irrevocable trust, do I still need the living trust I set up for estate planning and probate avoidance?*

   A: Yes. While assets that are transferred out of your name may not be included in your estate at your death, if you own in your name any portion of the corporations, partnerships, or other entities used in your asset protection plan, then those interests may be subject to probate. If you own the interests in the entities in the name of your living trust, those interests may generally be transferred to your heirs without the time and expense of the probate process.

8. Q: *My spouse is not a U.S. citizen, and I've heard that a trust may not work for us. Are there any additional challenges in using trusts for non U.S. citizens?*

   A: Yes. For estate planning purposes, your trust should have additional provisions so it qualifies as a qualified domestic trust (also known as a Q-DoT Trust). Ask your attorney about the need for and nature of these additional provisions.

9. Q: *I have a subchapter S corporation I would like to put into my trust, but I've heard there may be problems doing that. Is there any way for my corporation to be in my trust?*

   A: Yes. You can do one of two things. First, you could revoke your subchapter S election and return your corporation to subchapter C status, in which case its stock could be placed in and owned by your trust. Or, you could draft your trust so it contains the language necessary to qualify as a subchapter S corporation trust. See your attorney about the need for and nature of these provisions.

10. Q: *My wife and I live in a community property state, and we each own separate and community property assets. Is it possible to put those assets into an asset protection trust without changing their separate or community property nature?*

   A: Yes. Although state laws may vary, it is generally possible to allow the property you contribute to a trust to maintain its separate or community property status. Your trust will need to contain provisions stating that community property retains its community property character and separate property retains its separate property character, despite its transfer into the trust.

Quick Quiz—Should You Use a Foreign Trust in Your Asset Protection Plan?

The following quiz is designed to help you determine whether a foreign trust is right for you. As a general rule of thumb, you can almost always benefit from a domestic revocable living trust for probate avoidance. If your answers to the questions below indicate that a foreign trust is right for you, then you should consider using both types of trust in your asset protection plan. If not, a domestic trust is probably all you need.

1. Do you have liquid assets of more than $100,000? __ Yes __ No

2. Do you have $10,000 or more to spend on setting up and implementing a foreign component to your asset protection plan? __ Yes __ No

3. Are you prepared to spend $1,500 - $5,000 per year to maintain your foreign trusts and nominees, if any? __ Yes __ No

4. Are you willing to file all of the necessary documents with the Internal Revenue Service when establishing the foreign component to your asset protection plan? __ Yes __ No

5. Are you willing to accept the risk of having your assets in stable but uninsured banks? __ Yes __ No

6. Can you afford to wait 10–15 days to access your foreign representatives for signatures on documents and the like? __ Yes __ No

7. Can you afford to wait for U. S. checks (up to four weeks) or wires (five to fifteen days) to be processed through to your foreign accounts? __ Yes __ No

8. Are you willing to periodically travel to the country where you will establish your foreign trust? __ Yes __ No

9. Are you willing to prepare the extra tax returns and filings associated with having a foreign trust? __ Yes __ No

10. Are you comfortable with an aggressive tax and asset protection strategy? __ Yes __ No

Scoring: Unless you answered yes to all ten of the questions above, a foreign trust is probably not right for you, and you should consider other trust options. People who use foreign trusts for asset protection planning and tax reduction must be willing to take and defend an aggressive tax position with the Internal Revenue Service. They must be willing to complete all reporting and compliance filings when the trust is created and as it continues to operate. Delays of ten to fifteen days for transaction processing and up to four weeks for check clearing must be acceptable when dealing with overseas banks and representatives. If you aren't comfortable with or can't afford to have such delays, you should avoid the use of a foreign trust.

However, for those who can deal with the extra complications of having a foreign trust, the asset protection benefits can be substantial. While no plan is ever completely risk free, plans that use foreign trusts do offer the greatest protection for your assets. If you answered no to only one or two of the questions above, go back and consider your answers to those questions again. If on second look you still answer no, don't use a foreign trust.

Chapter Nine

Advantages and Disadvantages of Major Offshore Financial Centers Used in Asset Protection Planning

This chapter examines the major advantages and disadvantages of using entities based in fifteen of the most popular countries for asset protection planning. Because of the changing nature of foreign laws, it is wise to check with an attorney familiar with the laws of the country or countries in which you are considering forming your asset protection entities to find out how those laws apply to your specific situation.

To assist you in learning the latest about each of these countries' laws, I can provide local contact information for attorneys, asset protection planners, banks, consultants, and/or trust companies in each of these countries through my office.

Bahamas

Issue	Advantage or Disadvantage
Bearer Shares	*Advantage*—Bearer shares permitted as are nominee shareholders.
Management	*Advantage*—Two directors required. Telephonic meetings permitted, and meetings may be conducted anywhere in world.
Audits and Other Hassles	*Disadvantage*—Annual returns required listing officers directors, managers, and location of registered offices.
Trusts	*Advantage*—Principal statute is Trustee Act of 1893 and Trust Act 1989. Trust laws generally based on laws of England. Fraudulent Dispositions Act 1991 permits asset protection trusts but also permits creditors to void the trust where it is intended to defraud. Statute of limitations for attacking trusts is two years after transfer of assets. Burden of proof is on plaintiff to show that the person creating the trust knew of the specific claim and intended to commit a fraud.
Tax System	*Advantage*—No corporate, personal income, capital gains, profits, sales, inheritance, or estate taxes. No withholding taxes on dividends, interest, royalties, or payroll taxes. No taxes on foreign earned income.
Infrastructure	*Advantage*—Stable: Became independent nation within the Commonwealth of Nations, July 10, 1973. Executive power vested in Queen of England who appoints a Governor-General with the advice of the Prime Minister. Tripartite political system with Ministerial Cabinet, Parliament, and Senate.
Tax Treaties	*Advantage*—Not a party to double taxation agreement. Mutual Legal Assistance Treaties have been signed with United States, Canada, and United Kingdom regarding access to Bahamian bank accounts of suspected drug smugglers or blatant tax evaders.

Barbados

Issue	Advantage or Disadvantage
Bearer Shares	*Advantage*—Permitted
Management	*Advantage*—One director required. Meetings can be held outside Barbados, but minutes must be kept in Barbados.
Audits and Other Hassles	*Disadvantage*—Annual audits by an independent auditor who is a member of the Institute of Chartered Accountants of Barbados is required. Audited financial statements must be filed with Registrar of Companies and are available for public inspection. Private companies with gross revenues or gross assets of less than $BA 1 million are exempt from the audit and filing requirements.
Trusts	*Advantage*—English common law is complemented by Barbados Trustee Act. Protectors are permitted. Registration generally not required. Trust migration (moving the trust to another country) is permitted.
Tax System	*Disadvantage*—Individuals resident and domiciled in Barbados are subject to tax rates ranging from 20–50 percent of income greater than $BA55,00. Withholding applies to salaries and wages. Corporations resident in Barbados are taxed at standard 35 percent rate, subject to exceptions. Non-resident corporations taxed at 15 percent on Barbados sourced dividend, interest, royalty, and management fee income. No capital gains taxes. 15 percent sales tax on rooms, food, beverages, restaurant, and some clubs and 8 percent on non-business premises and cars. No estate, inheritance, and gift taxes.
Infrastructure	*Advantage*—Stable: Well-established political system with two parties. Queen of England appoints Governor-General. Has had democratic representative government since 1639. Member of British Commonwealth.
Tax Treaties	*Advantage*—Maintains double taxation treaties with Canada, Denmark, Norway, Sweden, Switzerland, United Kingdom, and United States.

Bermuda

Issue	Advantage or Disadvantage
Bearer Shares	*Disadvantage*—Not permitted, although nominee and corporate shareholders are permitted.
Management	*Disadvantage*—Two directors required as minimum and at least Two directors must be Bermuda residents (some exceptions apply). List of directors, available for public inspection, must be maintained. Meetings, which may be telephonic, may take place anywhere in the world.
Audits and Other Hassles	*Advantage*—No publicly filed audits required.
Trusts	*Advantage*—Trustee Act of 1975 controls and is based on English law. Trusts Act 1989 permits asset protection trusts for protection against legal claims of spouses, dependents, heirs, and creditors. Registration not required. Publicly filed audits not required.
Tax System	*Advantage*—No income, corporate, capital gains, wealth, or inheritance tax on income profits, dividends, or wealth. No withholding taxes.
Infrastructure	*Advantage*—Stable: Bermuda is a self-governing pursuant to the Bermuda Constitutional Order. A Queen-of-England-appointed Governor holds executive powers.
Tax Treaties	*Disadvantage*—No tax treaties with other countries for double taxation relief. 1988 treaty with United States permits exchange of information when requested, subject certain restrictions.

British Virgin Islands
IBC Companies Only

Issue	Advantage or Disadvantage
Bearer Shares	*Advantage*—Permitted.
Management	*Advantage*—One director required. Meetings outside of the country permitted. Telephonic meetings permitted.
Audits and Other Hassles	*Advantage*—Audits not generally required.
Trusts	*Advantage*—English law governs as amended by Trustee Ordinance CAP 260 of 1961 and Trustee Act 1993. One-hundred year perpetuity period. Protectors permitted. Exempt from British Virgin Island taxation.
Tax System	*Advantage*—Individuals taxed at rates from 3–20 percent. No tax to corporations registered under International Business Companies Act 1984, which most foreign corporations are.
Infrastructure	*Advantage*—Stable: British Virgin Islands is a British Protected Territory that became self-governing in 1967. Governed by Executive Council consisting of Governor appointed by Foreign and Commonwealth Officer of the United Kingdom, Chief Minister, three members of the Legislative Council, and Attorney General.
Tax Treaties	*Disadvantage*—British Virgin Islands maintains an exchange of information treaty with United States regarding criminal matters.

Cayman Islands

Issue	Advantage or Disadvantage
Bearer Shares	*Advantage*—Permitted.
Management	*Advantage*—One director, corporate secretary required. Secretary may be corporation.
Audits and Other Hassles	*Advantage*—Audits not generally required.
Trusts	*Disadvantage*—Long statue of limitations. Governed by Trusts Law 1987. One hundred year period permitted. Fraudulent Dispositions Law 1989 provides that to set aside a disposition, the creditor bears the burden of proving intent to defraud within six years of date of disposition being challenged.
Tax System	*Advantage*—No income, corporate, capital gains, wealth, or inheritance taxes.
Infrastructure	*Advantage*—British Colony.
Tax Treaties	*Disadvantage*—No tax treaties with other countries. Treaty with United States signed, facilitating the exchange of information where serious crime is involved.

Cook Islands

Issue	Advantage or Disadvantage
Bearer Shares	*Advantage*—Bearer shares permitted as are share warrants.
Management	*Advantage*—One Director required. Corporate directors permitted. Secretary required—must also be resident and a trustee company or officer of a trustee company.
Audits and Other Hassles	*Advantage*—Audit not required, but annual return must generally be filed.
Trusts	*Advantage*—Registration not required.
Tax System	*Advantage*—Non-resident companies registered under the Domestic Companies Act 1971-72 are not subject to tax except on Cook Islands sourced income. International companies registered under the International Companies Act 1981-82 are exempt from taxation.
Infrastructure	*Advantage*—Stable: Gained independence from New Zealand in 1965.
Tax Treaties	*Advantage*—Although the legal question of just what tax treaties the Cook Islands has is uncertain for reasons beyond the scope of this book. The Cook Islands government has indicated that it does not consider that it has any tax treaty agreements with any other country.

Gibraltar

Issue	Advantage or Disadvantage
Bearer Shares	*Advantage*—Bearer shares permitted as are nominees.
Management	*Advantage*—Only one director generally required. Corporations may be directors.
Audits and Other Hassles	*Disadvantage*—Annual audit and annual return filing required with Registrar Company.
Trusts	*Advantage*—Based on English common law and Trustee Act of 1893, Variations of Trusts Act 1958, English Laws Ordinance 1970, and Trusts Ordinance 1990, among other laws. Registration not required, but asset protection trusts get extra protection if they register transfer of assets with the Financial Services Commission. Trustees of APT's must be licensed by the FSC. Properly created and registered APT's cannot be voided under the Fraudulent Conveyances Act.
Tax System	*Advantage*—Resident companies taxed at 35 percent. Non-resident companies only taxed on Gibraltar sourced income.
Infrastructure	*Advantage*—Stable: Crown colony of England since 1713.
Tax Treaties	*Advantage*—No tax treaties maintained with any country.

Guernsey

Issue	Advantage or Disadvantage
Bearer Shares	*Disadvantage*—Not permitted.
Management	*Advantage*—Normally two directors. Meetings may be held anywhere.
Audits and Other Hassles	*Disadvantage*—Annual audits are required, although no public filings of financial statements are required.
Trusts	*Advantage*—controlled by Trusts Law 1989. Registration not required.
Tax System	*Disadvantage*—20 percent tax on world-wide income. Tax returns required. International companies pay taxes on Guernsey sourced income.
Infrastructure	*Advantage*—Stable: Not part of United Kingdom but are autonomous possessions of English Crown.
Tax Treaties	*Advantage*—Policy is to avoid entering into tax treaties. Maintains treaties with United Kingdom and with Jersey.

Hong Kong

Issue	Advantage or Disadvantage
Bearer Shares	*Disadvantage*—Two shareholders required, no more than fifty permitted. Nominee shareholders permitted.
Management	*Disadvantage*—Two Directors required and a secretary. Secretary must reside in Hong Kong.
Audits and Other Hassles	*Disadvantage*—Audit required.
Trusts	N/A
Tax System	*Advantage*—Only Hong Kong sourced profits are subject to tax.
Infrastructure	*Disadvantage*—Stable, but future uncertain: British Crown Colony founded in 1841. New Territories were subject of a lease from China that expired June 30, 1997. On July 1, 1997, Hong Kong reverted to China and became a special administrative region under authority of Central People's Government of China. Under a Joint Declaration entered into by China and the United Kingdom, it is proposed that the social, legal, and economic systems of Hong Kong remain unchanged for fifty years after 1997.
Tax Treaties	*Advantage*—No tax treaties.

Isle of Man

Issue	Advantage or Disadvantage
Bearer Shares	*Advantage*—Permitted.
Management	*Advantage*—Two directors required. Secretary required and may be required to have an Isle of Man work permit.
Audits and Other Hassles	*Disadvantage*—Annual audits with qualified auditor required.
Trusts	*Advantage*—Governed by Trustee Act 1961 and Variation of Trusts Act 1961.
Tax System	*Advantage*—Non-resident companies which file a non-resident declaration with the Registrar of Companies in Isle of Man under the Non-Resident Company Duty Act of 1986 only pay taxes on Isle of Man sourced income.
Infrastructure	*Advantage*—Stable: Independent.
Tax Treaties	*Advantage*—Isle of Man has only one tax treaty on double taxation avoidance with the United Kingdom made in 1955.

Jersey

Issue	Advantage or Disadvantage
Bearer Shares	*Disadvantage*—Not permitted.
Management	*Disadvantage*—One director required for private company. Secretary required. Corporations may not be directors.
Audits and Other Hassles	*Advantage*—Audits not required to be publicly filed.
Trusts	*Advantage*—Governed by the Trusts Law 1984.
Tax System	*Advantage*—See Guernsey.
Infrastructure	*Advantage*—Stable: Not a part of the United Kingdom. An autonomous possession of the British Crown.
Tax Treaties	*Advantage*—Policy to not enter into tax treaties, and only has treaties with France, Guernsey, and United Kingdom.

Nevis

Issue	Advantage or Disadvantage
Bearer Shares	*Advantage*—Permitted.
Management	*Advantage*—Directors may be nominee and corporations.
Audits and Other Hassles	*Advantage*—None required.
Trusts	*Advantage*—Governed by Nevis International Exempt Trust Ordinance 1994.
Tax System	*Advantage*—No taxes for qualified companies.
Infrastructure	*Advantage*—Stable: Gained independence in 1983 and is a member of the Federation of St. Kitts, Nevis, and Anguilla.
Tax Treaties	*Advantage*—Double taxation avoidance treaty with the United Kingdom.

Panama

Issue	Advantage or Disadvantage
Bearer Shares	*Advantage*—Permitted.
Management	*Disadvantage*—Three directors and officers required. Need not be Panama residents, but identity must be filed with the Public Registrar.
Audits and Other Hassles	*Advantage*—No audits required by law.
Trusts	*Disadvantage*—Governed by the Trust Law 1984, which took forty years to implement due to the uncertain political nature of the country.
Tax System	*Advantage*—Panama sourced income only is taxed.
Infrastructure	*Disadvantage*—Unstable. Republic of Panama is an independent state with an uncertain political climate.
Tax Treaties	*Advantage*—No tax treaties with any other country, though Panama has an investment protection treaty with China to protect the investments of Chinese citizens in Panama.

Turks and Caicos

Issue	Advantage or Disadvantage
Bearer Shares	*Advantage*—Permitted.
Management	*Advantage*—Only one director required, as is a secretary. Directors and secretaries may be corporations.
Audits and Other Hassles	*Advantage*—Audits generally not required.
Trusts	*Advantage*—Governed by the Trusts Ordinance 1990 based on Jersey legislation and other countries trust laws. Asset protection trusts permitted and attacking creditors must prove insolvency of the person creating the trust at the time that the trust was created.
Tax System	*Advantage*—No income, corporate, withholding, capital gains, profits, or assets taxes.
Infrastructure	*Advantage*—Stable: British dependency.
Tax Treaties	*Advantage*—No tax treaties with foreign countries. It is a party to a Mutual Legal Assistance Treaty between the United Kingdom and the United States, to facilitate the exchange of information where serious crime is involved. The treaty does not extend to the exchange of information on tax offenses or those that are purely tax related.

Chapter Ten

Sample Asset Protection Plan Designs

While there are thousands of possible combinations of the various asset protection planning entities to fit the vast variety of situations, the asset protection objectives of many individuals are the same. The sample asset protection plans provided in this chapter are intended to serve as guides to how you might combine the various ideas, strategies, tools, and techniques provided in this book to accomplish your particular asset protection planning objectives. While none of the sample plans is likely to be absolutely perfect for your situation, one or more of the plans should provide you with a template to tailor to your individual needs. As always, remember to pay close attention to any limitations on your ability to transfer assets into your asset protection plan, as discussed more fully earlier in this book.

Simple Domestic Plan to Protect a Family Home

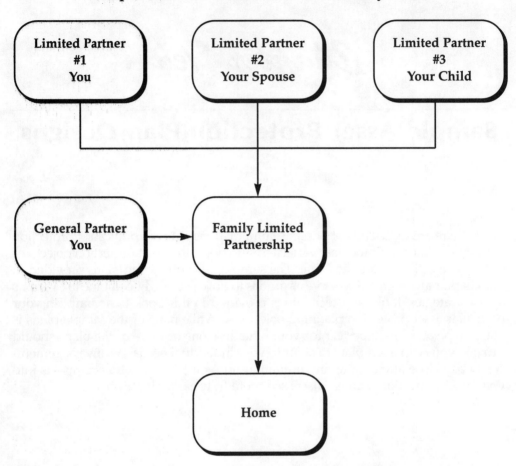

Simple Domestic Plan for an Unmarried Person

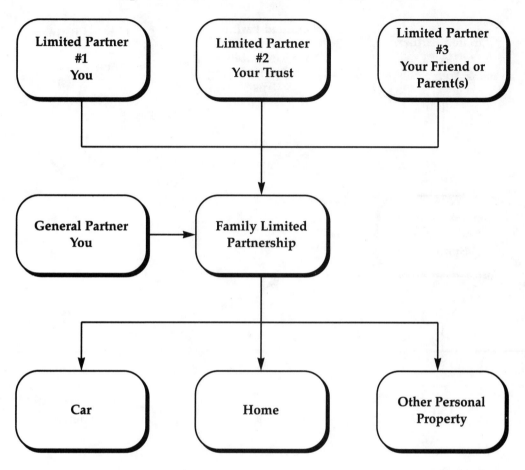

Simple Domestic Plan for a Married Couple without Children

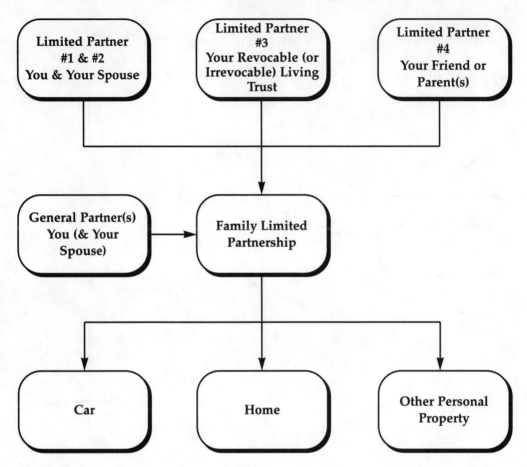

Simple Domestic Plan for a Married Couple with Children

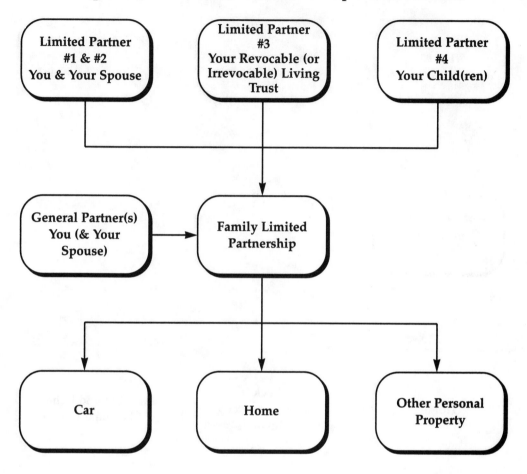

Simple Domestic Plan for a Business Owner

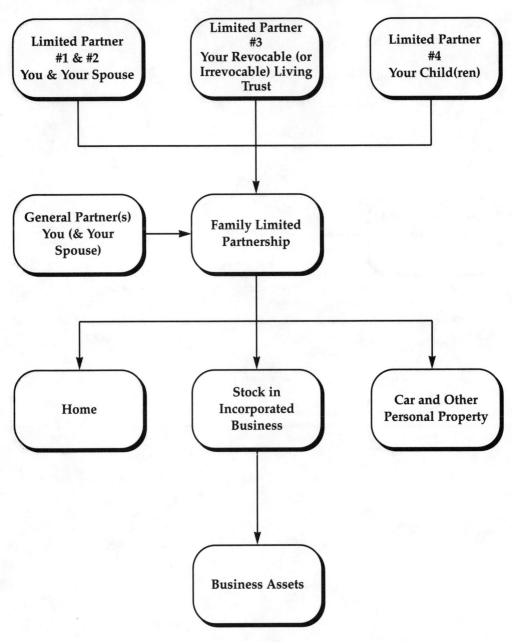

Complex Foreign Plan to Protect a Family Home

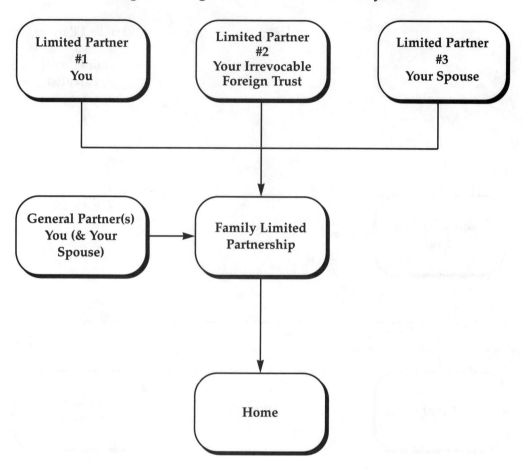

Complex Foreign Plan for an Unmarried Person

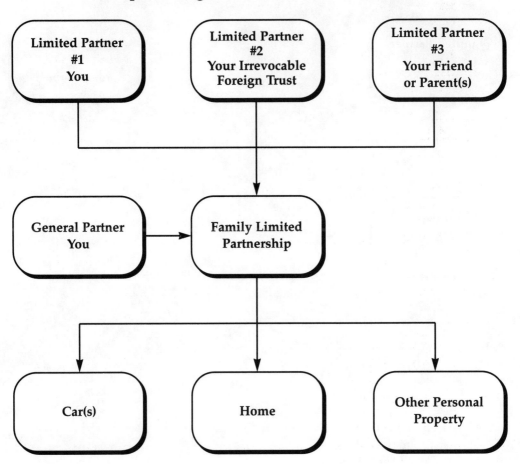

Complex Foreign Plan for a Married Couple without Children

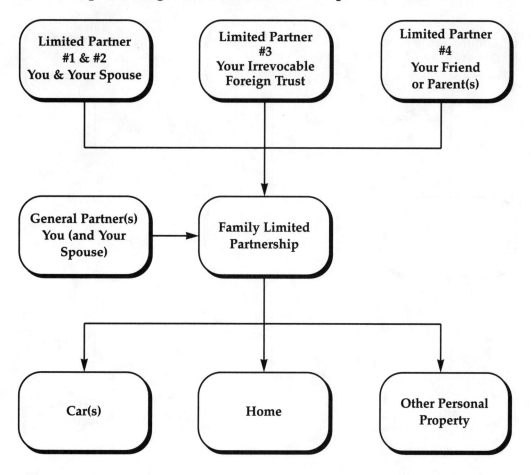

Complex Foreign Plan for a Married Couple with Children

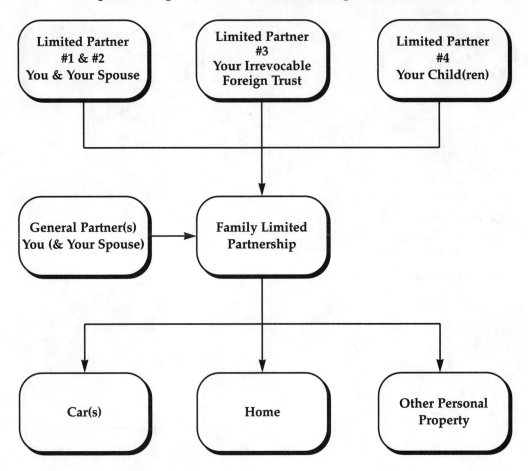

Complex Foreign Plan for a Business Owner

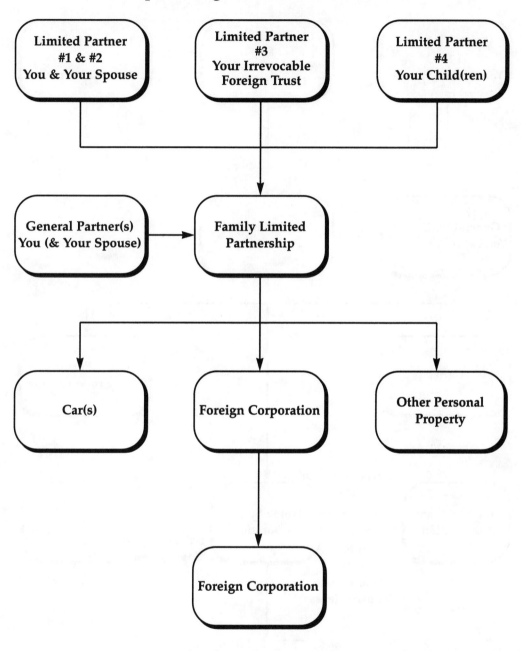

State Income Tax Reduction Plan

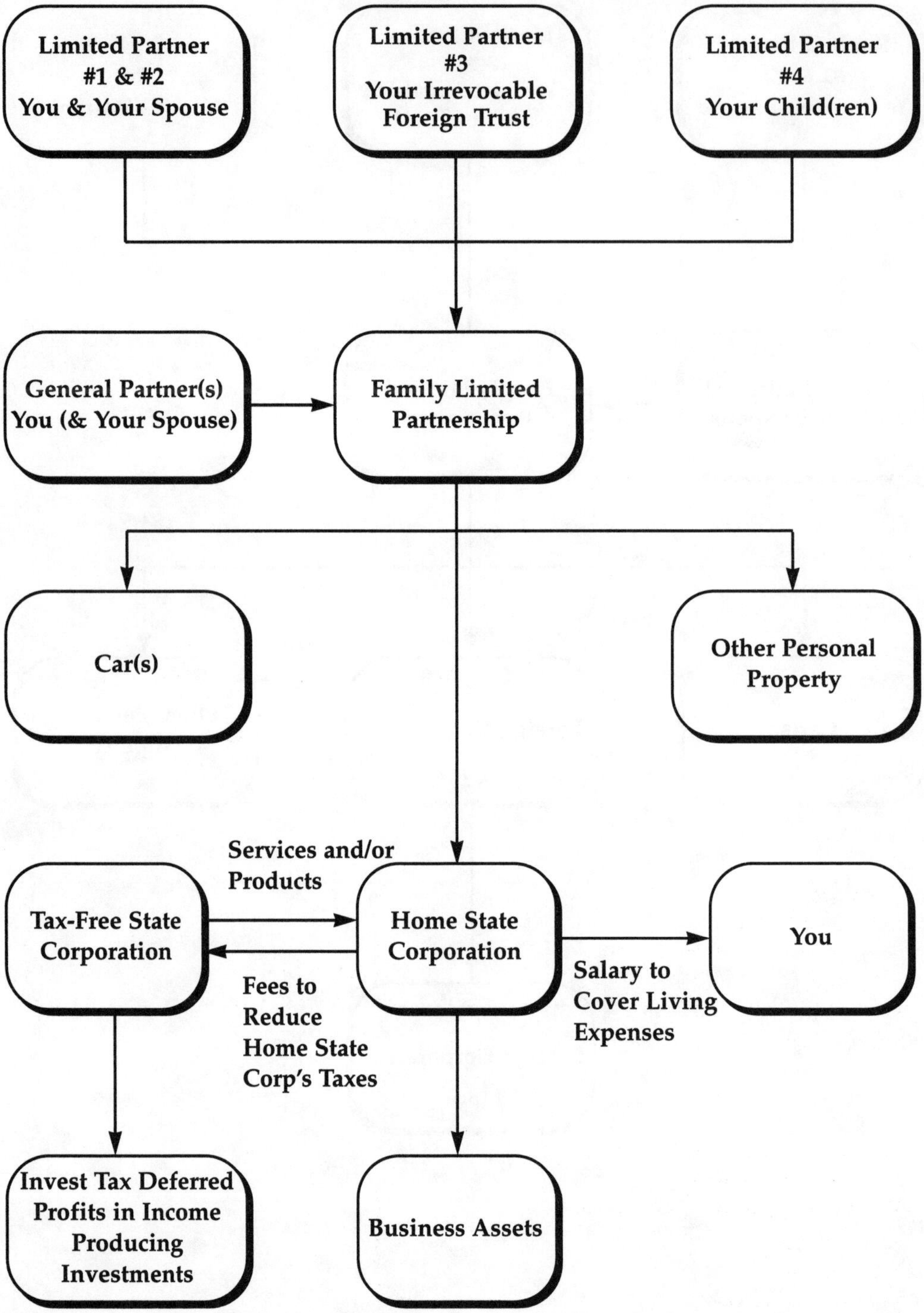

Limited Partner
#1 & #2
You & Your Spouse

Limited Partner
#3
Your Irrevocable
Foreign Trust

Limited Partner
#4
Your Child(ren)

General Partner(s)
You (& Your Spouse)

Family Limited
Partnership

Car(s)

Other Personal
Property

Services and/or
Products

Tax-Free State
Corporation

Home State
Corporation

You

Fees to
Reduce
Home State
Corp's Taxes

Salary to
Cover Living
Expenses

Invest Tax Deferred
Profits in Income
Producing
Investments

Business Assets

State and Federal Income Tax Reduction Plan

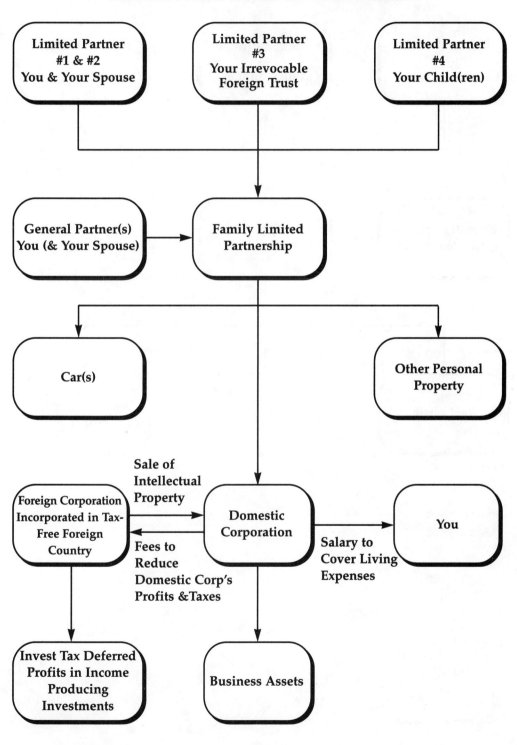

Estate Tax Reduction Plan

```
┌─────────────────┐   ┌─────────────────┐   ┌─────────────────┐
│ Limited Partner │   │ Limited Partner │   │ Limited Partner │
│    #1 & #2      │   │       #3        │   │       #4        │
│ You & Your      │   │ Your Children   │   │ Your Other Heirs│
│    Spouse       │   │                 │   │                 │
└─────────────────┘   └─────────────────┘   └─────────────────┘
```

```
┌─────────────────┐   ┌─────────────────┐
│ General         │   │ Family Limited  │
│ Partner(s)      │ → │ Partnership     │
│ You (& Your     │   │                 │
│ Spouse)         │   │                 │
└─────────────────┘   └─────────────────┘
```

```
┌─────────────────┐   ┌─────────────────┐   ┌─────────────────┐
│  Real Estate    │   │ Business        │   │ Other Personal  │
│                 │   │ Interests       │   │ Property        │
└─────────────────┘   └─────────────────┘   └─────────────────┘
```

Plan for Intellectual Property Owners

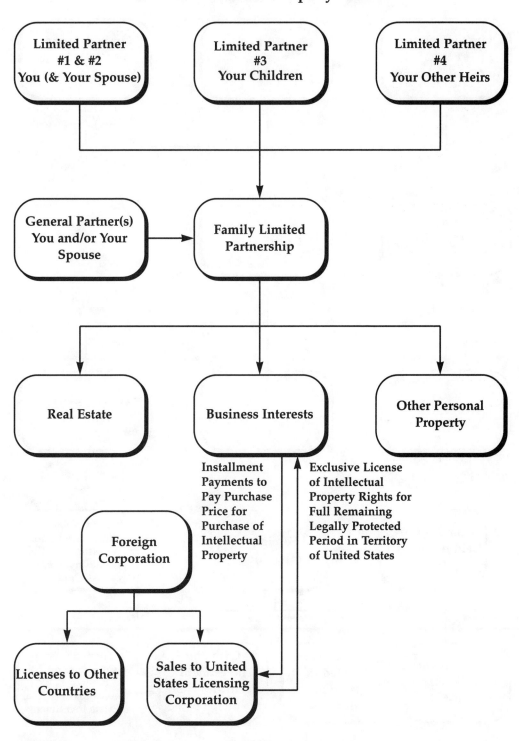

Plan for Those Engaged in High Risk Occupations

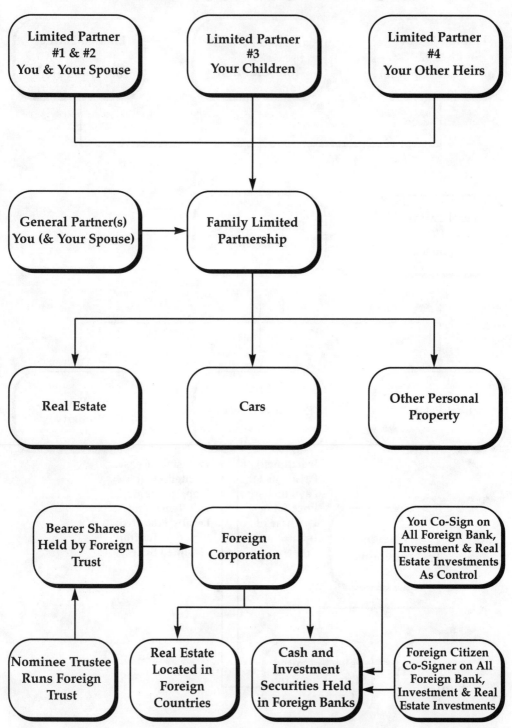

Plan for Celebrities

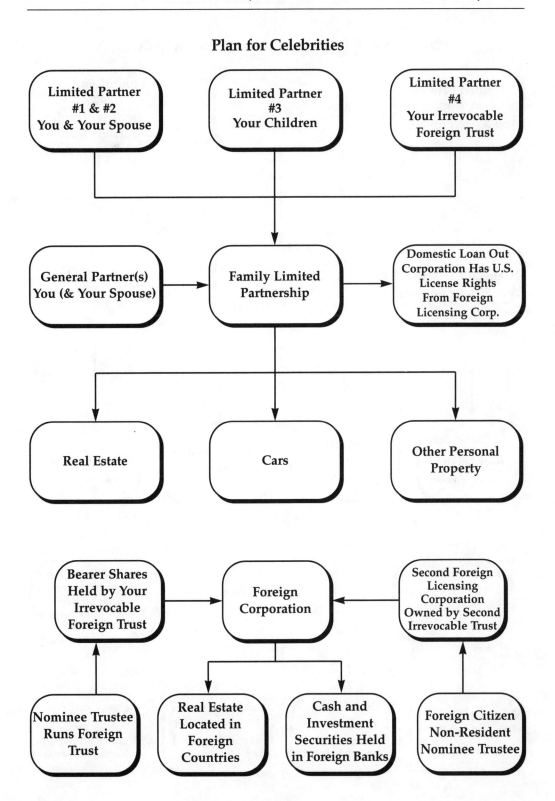

Plan for Stock Promoters and Investment Advisors

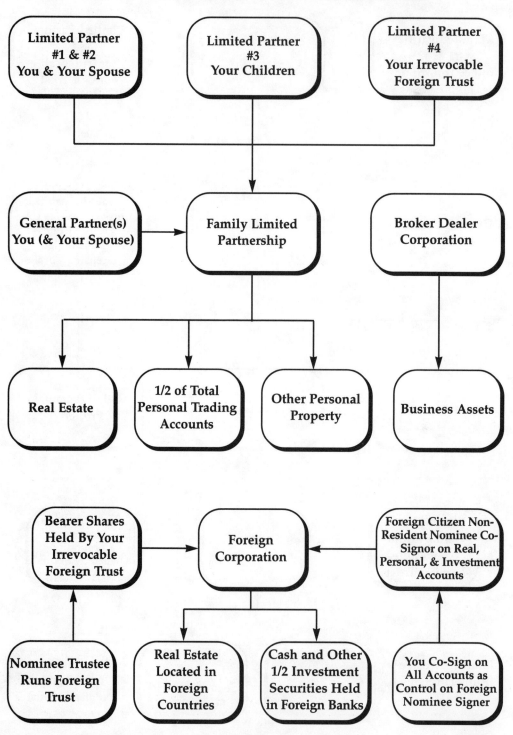

Plan for Doctors

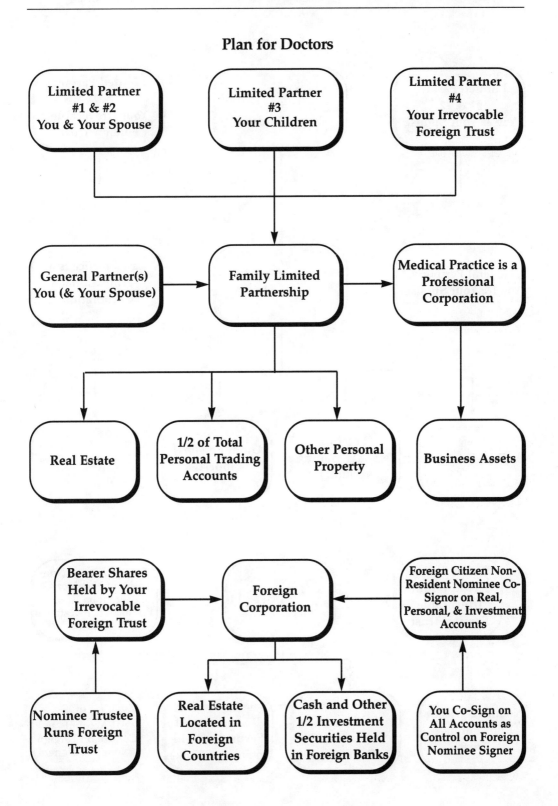

Plan for Attorneys

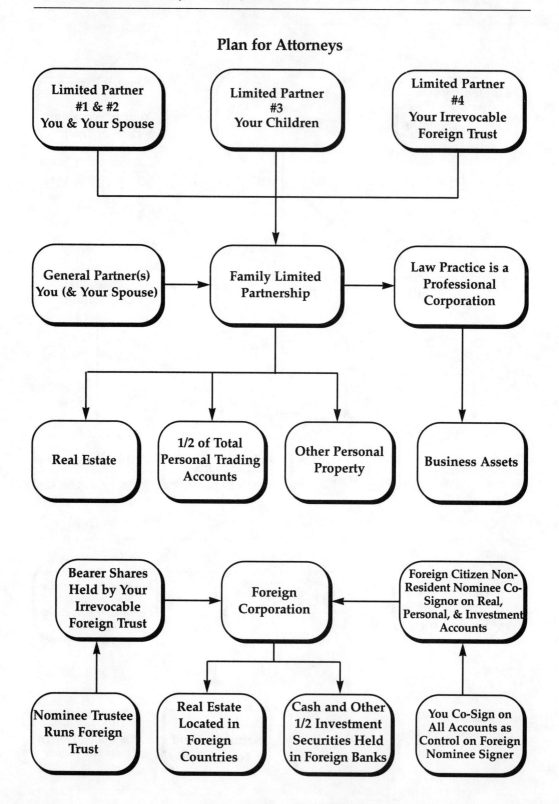

Chapter Eleven

Managing the Plan, Keeping It Funded and Protected

One of the most common mistakes people make after designing their asset protection plan is failing to properly implement it so it provides them with all the benefits that caused them to design it in the first place. No matter how much planning you do, no matter how beautifully designed and cleverly crafted your asset protection plan is, it will do absolutely no good if it is not properly implemented as well. This chapter is designed to assist you in getting your plan up and running so you can enjoy the benefits of all the design work you did.

Transferring Assets to the Plan

Once you have designed your asset protection plan, formed all of the partnerships, corporations, trusts, and other entities that the plan comprises, and retained the services of whoever will assist you in operating those entities, the next step is to begin the process of transferring your assets into the plan. These transfers are usually accomplished in specific ways, using specific documents, depending on the types of assets being transferred. Table 15 provides a summary of the most common methods for transferring various assets into your asset protection plan.

Table 15
Documents Typically Used to Transfer Assets into Asset Protection Plans

Asset	Transfer Document
Bank Accounts, Money Market Accounts, Certificates of Deposit	Your bank should have the necessary pre-printed forms to transfer these assets into your new asset protection entities. Ask your banker for the appropriate forms.
Notes and Accounts Receivable	These assets are generally transferred by an assignment of all of your right, title, and interest in the note or receivable to your new asset protection entity. A sample form of assignment is provided following this table.
Stocks, Bonds, Mutual Funds, and Other Securities (Including Stock Held in Small or Family Owned Corporations)	These assets are generally transferred in one of two ways. 1) Stocks and other securities held in a brokerage account or mutual fund can generally be transferred by simply changing the name on the account with your broker. Your broker should be able to provide you with the necessary forms to accomplish the transfers if you request them. 2) Small or family owned corporations and stock held in your name, where you hold the actual stock certificates, is generally transferred by endorsing the back of the stock certificate over to the name of your new asset protection entity and forwarding to the registrar or transfer agent for the corporation whose stock you are transferring. The transfer will then be entered on the stock transfer ledger of the corporation, and you will be issued a new certificate. This transfer may also be accomplished by using a stock power. (A sample stock power form is provided following this table.)
Automobiles, Recreational Vehicles, Mobile Homes, Boats, Planes, Other Registered Vehicles	These assets are generally transferred by completing the necessary forms provided by the Division of Motor Vehicles or other registering agency. Simply request these forms from the agency with which the asset is registered.
Miscellaneous Personal Property	These assets are generally transferred using a bill of sale and assignment. (A bill of sale and assignment form is provided following this table.)
Real Estate	Real estate is generally transferred to your asset protection entities using a quitclaim deed. This type of deed transfers whatever interest you have in the real property to your asset protection planning entity, and it may be used whether you own the asset individually or with other people. Because this type of deed only transfers the interest you own, you are the only one who needs to sign it. (A sample quitclaim deed form is provided following this table.)
Copyrights, Trademarks, and Patents	These types of intellectual property are generally transferred by an assignment filed and recorded with the United States Copyright Office or the Patent and Trademark Office. If you will be transferring this type of property, call the appropriate office and ask for the latest version of their forms.

Forms 4–7 are commonly used in transferring assets:

Form 4
Sample Assignment

ASSIGNMENT

As of this [list date], the undersigned [name of person transferring the asset] ("Seller") for valuable consideration, receipt of which is hereby acknowledged, does hereby grant, convey, sell, assign, and transfer over to [name of your new asset protection entity] ("Buyer") all of my right, title, and interest in and to the following described property:

[Describe the property being transferred into your asset protection plan.]

Title to all properties specified as being conveyed and transferred shall become fully and completely conveyed and transferred to the above-named [person, partnership, corporation, or whatever type of entity the asset(s) is/are being transferred to].

IN WITNESS WHEREOF, I have caused this bill of sale and assignment to be executed on [list date].

_____
[Name of Person Transferring the Asset]

CERTIFICATE OF ACKNOWLEDGMENT OF NOTARY PUBLIC

State of:_____

County of:_____

On [DATE], before me, [NAME OF NOTARY PUBLIC], personally appeared [NAME OF PERSON APPEARING], personally known to me (or proved to me on the basis of satisfactory evidence) to be the person(s) whose name(s) is/are subscribed to the within instrument and acknowledged to me that he/she/they executed the same in his/her/their authorized capacity(ies), and that by his/her/their signatures on the instrument the person(s), or the entity on behalf of which the person(s) acted, executed the instrument.

Witness my official hand and seal.

_____
Notary Public

Form 5
Sample Stock Power

STOCK POWER

FOR VALUE RECEIVED, [Name of Person Transferring Stock] hereby sells, assigns, and transfers unto [Name of Asset Protection Entity To Which the Stock Is Being Transferred], [Typed Number of Shared Being Transferred] ([Number of Shares Being Transferred]) Shares of the [Common/Preferred/Class A/Etc.] Capital Stock of the [Corporation/LLC/Etc.] standing in [Name of Person Transferring Stock]'s name on the books of said corporation represented by Certificate(s) No. [Stock Certificate Number] herewith and do irrevocably constitute and appoint [Leave Blank for Transfer Agent to Complete] as attorney-in-fact to transfer the said stock on the books of the within named corporation with full power of substitution in the premises.

Dated:_____   Signed by: _____

In the Presence of:_____

NOTICE: The signature in this assignment must correspond with the name as written on the face of the Certificate, in every particular, without alteration.

Signature Guaranteed by: _____

Form 6
Sample Bill of Sale and Assignment

BILL OF SALE AND ASSIGNMENT

This instrument is effective as of [Date] by [Name of Person Transferring Asset] (hereafter called "Assignor") and [Name of Asset Protection Entity To Which the Asset is Being Transferred], (hereafter called "Assignee").

For good and valuable consideration, the sufficiency, adequacy, and receipt of which is hereby acknowledged, Assignor hereby assigns, transfers, and conveys to Assignee all of Assignor's right, title, and interest in and to all of Assignor's tangible personal property. The term "tangible personal property" refers, without limitation, to such items as furniture, furnishings, silverware, objects of art, china, clothing, jewelry, sporting equipment, automobiles, books, collections of tangible personal property, and other tangible personal property normally kept at Assignor's residence(s). The term "tangible personal property" includes any insurance policies on this tangible personal property and any proceeds of these policies. The term "tangible personal property" excludes cash and other items of intangible personal property, even if represented by tangible documentation of ownership and also excludes tangible personal property used by the Assignor in a trade, business, or profession; gold bars; bars of other metals; and any other tangible property of an investment nature (other than art objects and collections of tangible personal property).

_____   _____
[Name of Person Transferring Asset]—Assignor   [Name of Asset Protection Entity]—Assignee

Form 7
Sample Quitclaim Deed

RECORDING REQUESTED BY /
MAIL TAX STATEMENTS TO:

[Name of Person Transferring the Property] and
[Name of any Co-Transferor]
[Street Address of Transferor(s)]
[City, State and Zip of Transferor(s)]

When recorded, return to:

[Name of Person Transferring the Property] and
[Name of any Co-Transferor]
[Street Address of Transferor(s)]
[City, State and Zip of Transferor(s)]

Tax Assessor's Parcel Number:

QUITCLAIM DEED

The undersigned quitclaimors declare: Documentary transfer tax is NONE. No consideration given—
Change in formal title only—See Note #1 below.

FOR NO CONSIDERATION, [Name(s) of Transferor(s) as stated on grant deed to property], do(es) hereby
REMISE, RELEASE, AND FOREVER QUITCLAIM to [Name of Asset Protection Entity to Which the
Property Is Being Transferred], all of [his/her/their] right, title, and interest in and to the following
described real property in the City of [City], County of [County], State of [State]:

[Legal Description As It Appears on Grant Deed for Property]

NOTE #1: *Conveyance transferring Quitclaimors' interest in a revocable living trust.* This conveyance transfers the Quitclaimors' interest into an entity owned by them and this is a change in formal title only, which is exempt from property tax reassessment.

Dated: [Date]

_____
[Signature of Person Transferring the Asset]

_____
[Signature of Co-Transferor, If Any]

CERTIFICATE OF ACKNOWLEDGMENT OF NOTARY PUBLIC

State of:_____

County of:_____

On [DATE], before me, [NAME OF NOTARY PUBLIC], personally appeared [NAME OF PERSON
APPEARING], personally known to me (or proved to me on the basis of satisfactory evidence) to be the
person(s) whose name(s) is/are subscribed to the within instrument and acknowledged to me that
he/she/they executed the same in his/her/their authorized capacity(ies), and that by his/her/their signatures on the instrument the person(s), or the entity on behalf of which the person(s) acted, executed the
instrument.

Witness my official hand and seal.

_____
Notary Public

Investing from within the Plan without Losing Benefits

Just as important as transferring the assets that you want to protect into your asset protection plan is keeping the income generated from those assets in the plan as you collect and reinvest it. To accomplish this, you should be certain that all transactions with any principal or income of assets that you have transferred into your asset protection plan are entered into by the person or persons who are in charge of and authorized to act on behalf of the applicable asset protection planning entities. Also be sure that the transactions are entered into in the name(s) of the appropriate asset protection entity(ies) and not in your name as an individual. There is no quicker way of losing your asset protection benefits than by carelessly operating outside your plan and commingling your personal and asset protection plan assets.

Defending the Plan from Attacks

The objective of your asset protection plan is to make you an unattractive target for litigation by giving you a low profile and making your assets more difficult for creditors to get to in the event that they do sue you and obtain a judgment. This won't always stop an aggressive creditor from chasing you as far as possible to collect on its claim. In the event that you face such a creditor, your asset protection plan may come under attack. If it does, then you should immediately seek the advice of a qualified litigation attorney. Your plan will provide you with leverage to settle your case, as well as protection from creditors who obtain judgments against you, but it is always wise to attempt to settle your creditor disputes as quickly as possible to avoid the headaches and expense of litigation. When this is not possible, use the protection you have created for your assets to its fullest extent and don't give away any more information about your asset protection plan than is absolutely necessary under the circumstances. As long as you followed the guidelines provided earlier in this book on the limitations and restrictions on asset protection planning, you shouldn't have any problem successfully defending your plan.

Keeping Up with Changing Treaties and Laws

The laws applicable to asset protection planning are changing rapidly. This is a relatively new area of the law, and legislatures, courts and juries in this country and abroad are refining and changing the rules at a rapid pace. It is important to stay informed as to what changes in these laws may affect you and the plan that you have put into place to protect your assets. Use your library, attorney, and reporting services to stay abreast of these developments as they occur and respond to them by making any adjustments to your asset protection as required.

Regular Tax and Related Reporting Compliance

As we discussed previously, you are required to file numerous forms with the Internal Revenue Service and other government agencies when you establish your asset protection plan and on a continuing basis thereafter. Don't forget to keep up with your annual filings once you have your asset protection plan in place. You can rest assured that the IRS won't forget. Additionally, be sure to pay any annual fees to consultants, nominees, advisors, and state, federal, and international government agencies that are required to keep your asset protection plan current and in good standing. Don't let all your hard work of designing and implementing your asset protection plan go to waste because of a failure to keep the plan active.

Conclusion

Tying It All Together

Now that you have read through this book in its entirety, you should have a clear idea of the steps, strategies, tools, and limits of asset protection planning. Armed with this knowledge, you must now take action to begin taking the steps necessary to design and implement your own asset protection plan to give you the peace of mind that can only come from knowing that your hard earned assets are completely protected from the claims of your creditors. Take action now to build a fortress around your wealth. Start your asset protection plan today.

Epilogue

Index

Epilogue

Where Do You Go from Here

If you need further information about the material contained in this book, please feel free to write me at:

> B. Roland Frasier, III
> Gage, Frasier & Teeple
> 9255 Towne Centre Dr., Suite 500
> San Diego, CA 92121-3038

You may also be interested in purchasing the companion to this book:

Complete Asset Protection Forms

Index

About the Author

As the nation's leading expert in the area of asset protection, B. Roland Frasier III, has designed or implemented asset protection plans for clients ranging from builders and developers to movie stars and well-known entertainment personalities. He is an attorney and partner in the law firm of Gage, Frasier & Teeple in San Diego, California. From $42 million bankruptcies to international public companies, Frasier has helped many clients structure their holdings to protect them against improper claims and losses. He is renowned for his creativity and innovation in designing plans to protect assets, reduce taxes, and structure complex domestic and international business operations. Frasier has published articles on asset protection and taxation, which appeared in the *San Diego Business Journal* and other media. He is frequently quoted as an authority on tax planning in newspapers and other publications.

Frasier holds a J.D. from California Western School of Law and a B.S. in accounting from Virginia Commonwealth University. He has been a member of the American Bar Association and the California Bar Association since 1990.